Pop Art New

Andreas Schröder
&
Eckhard Schmittner

Impressum

Titel: Pop Art New

© 2018 Andreas Schröder / Eckhard Schmittner

Alle Rechte vorbehalten.

Coverbild: Andreas Schröder

Covergestaltung: Eckhard Schmittner

Kontakt: schiri3@web.de

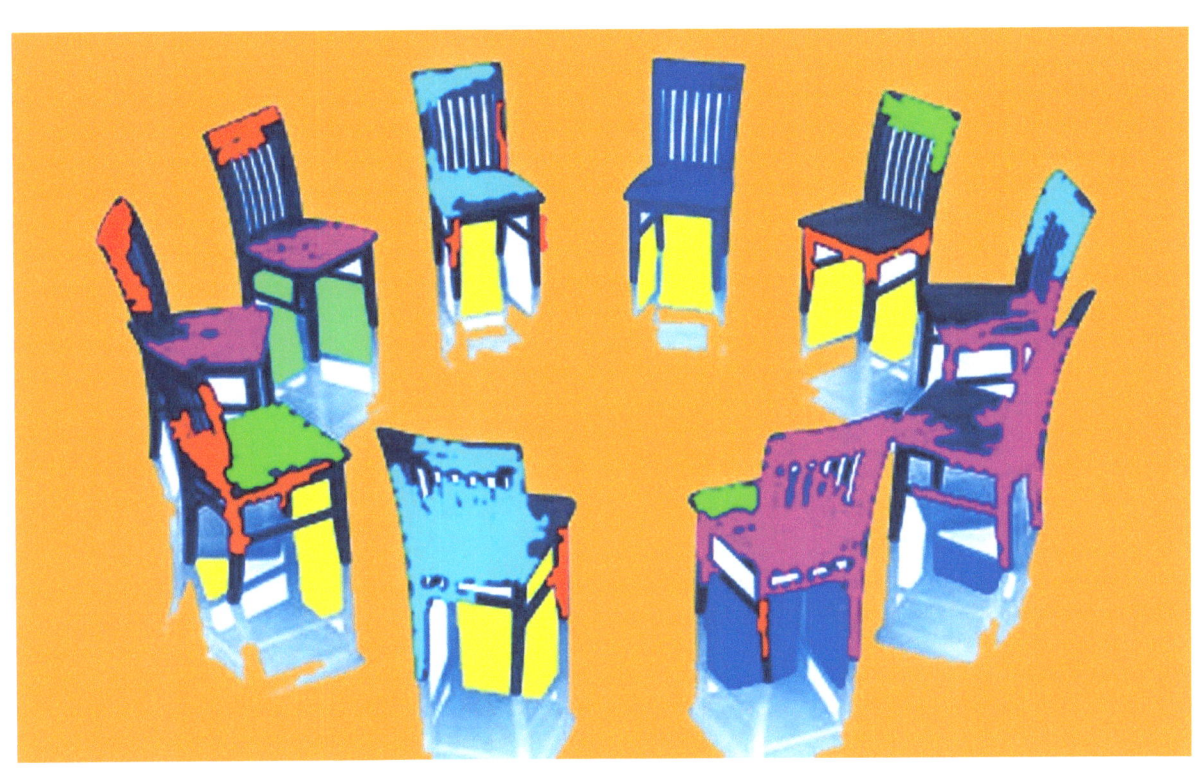

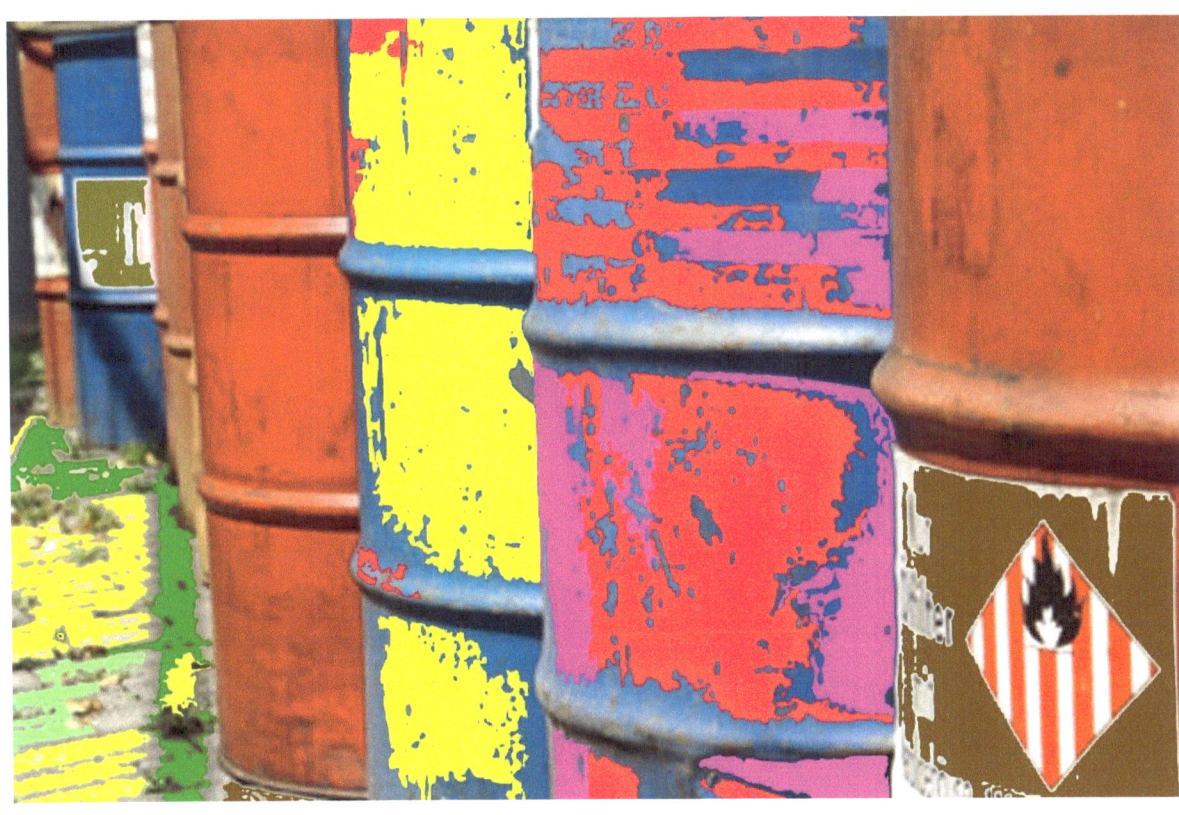

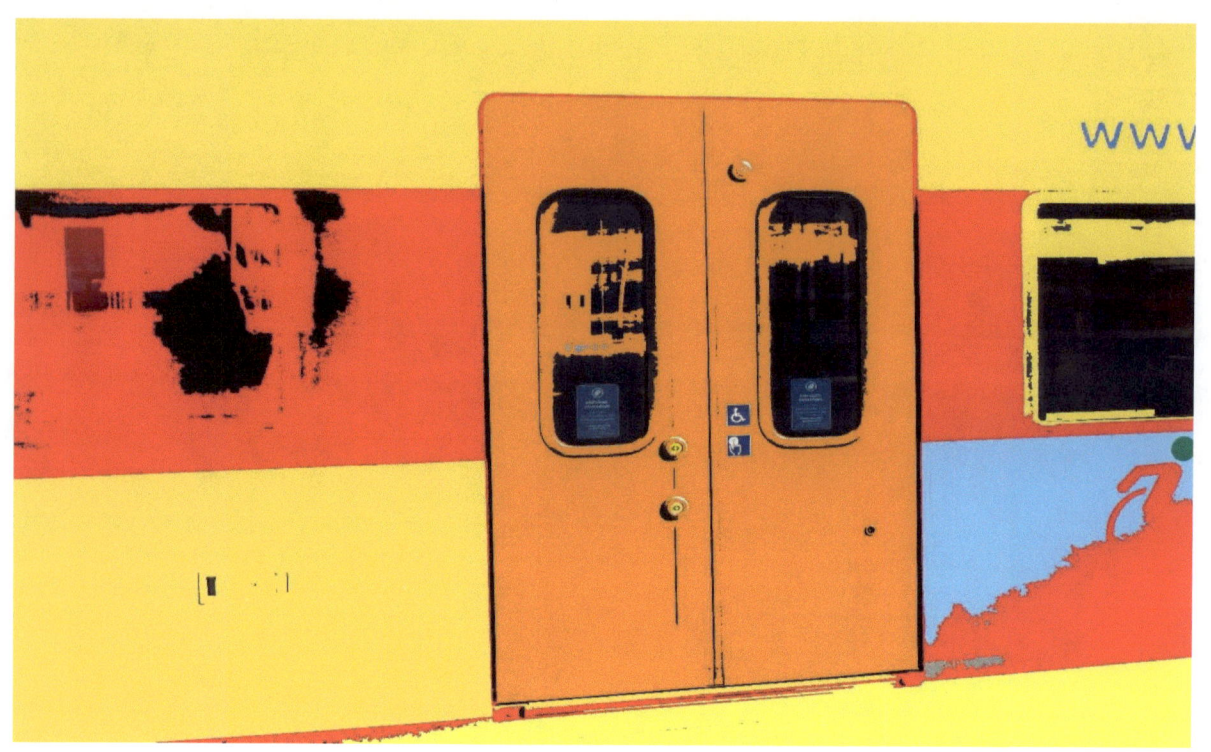
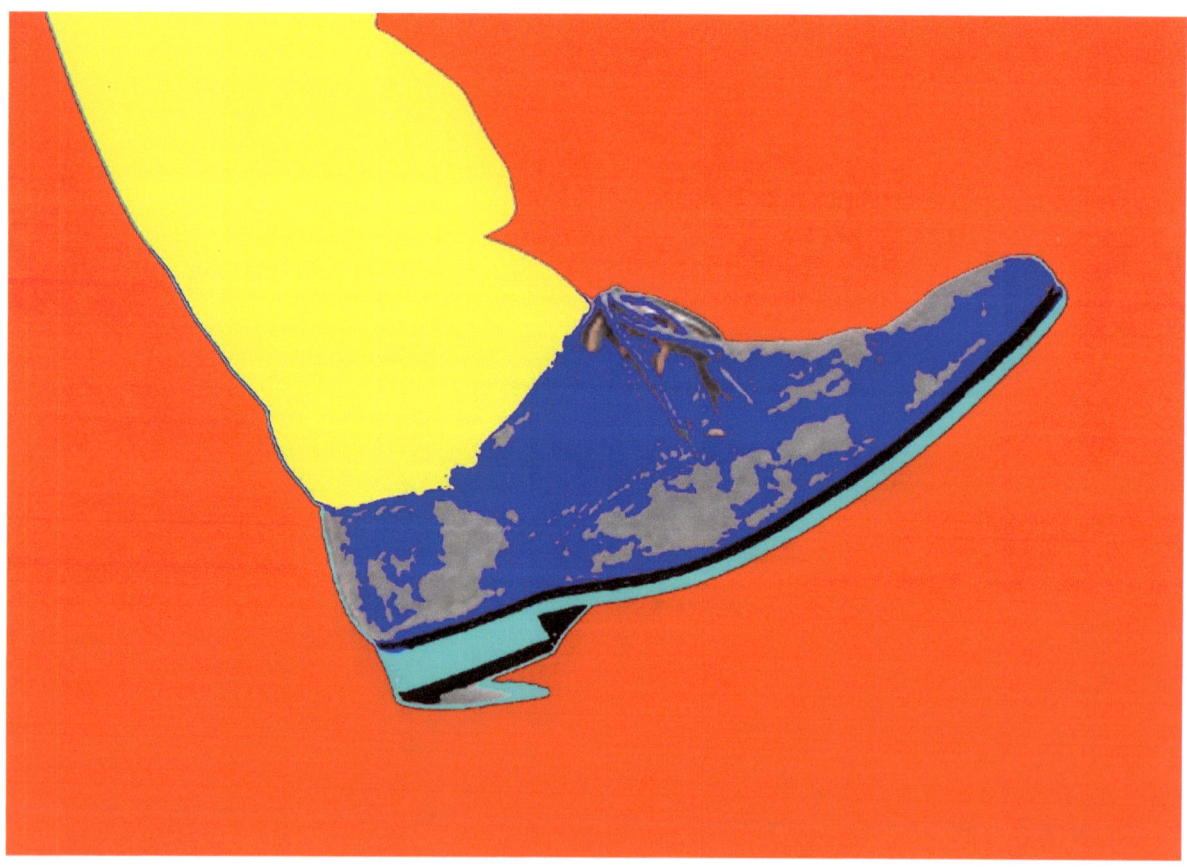

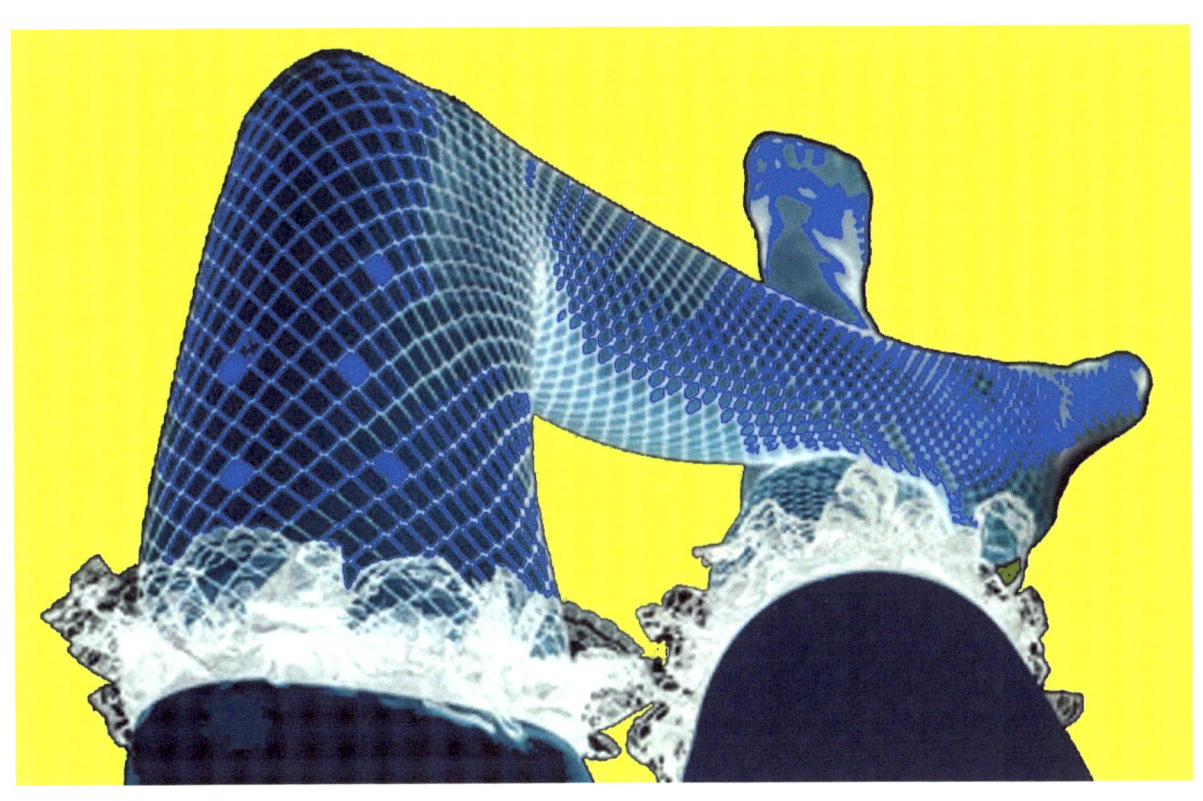
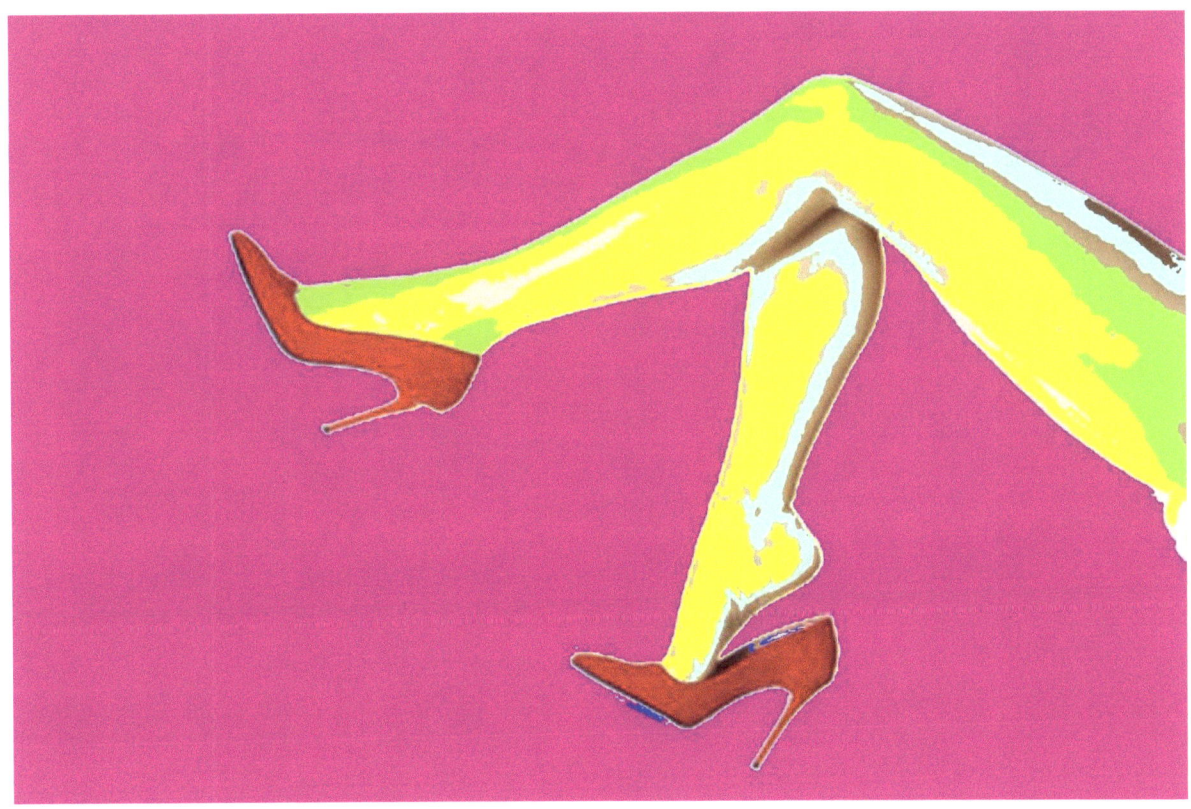

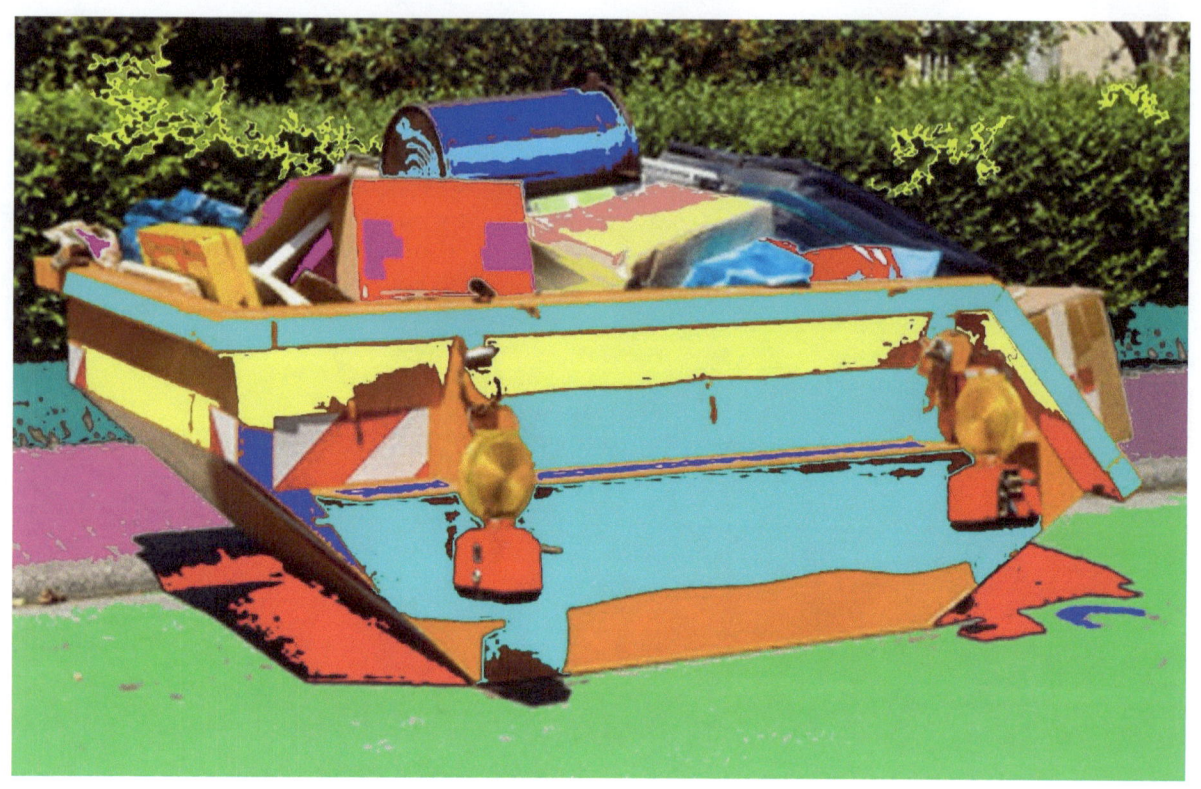
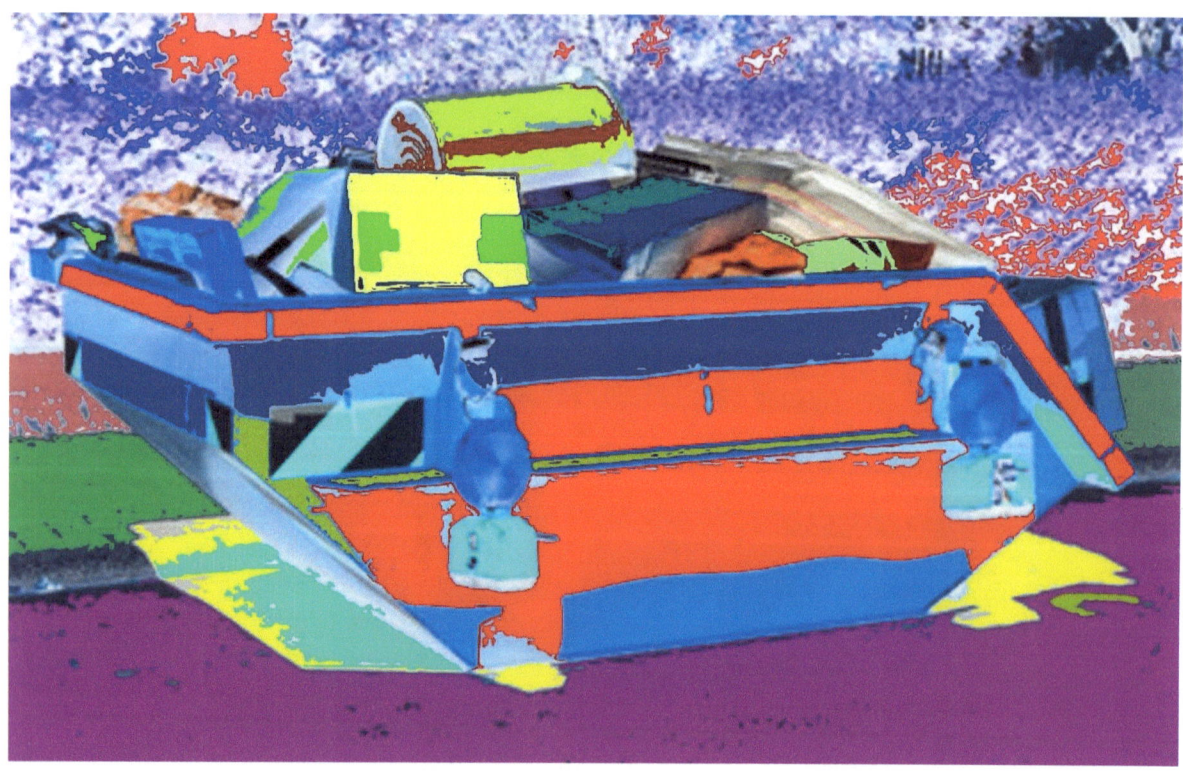

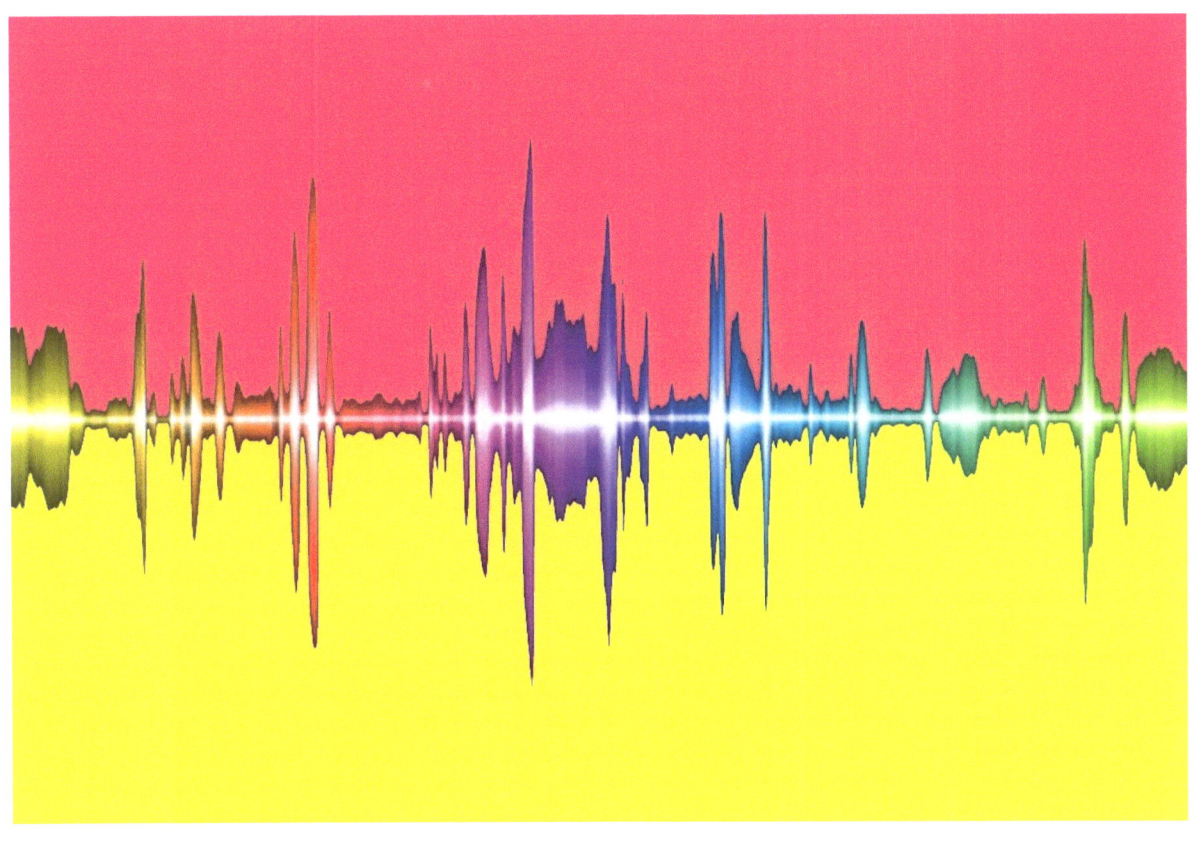
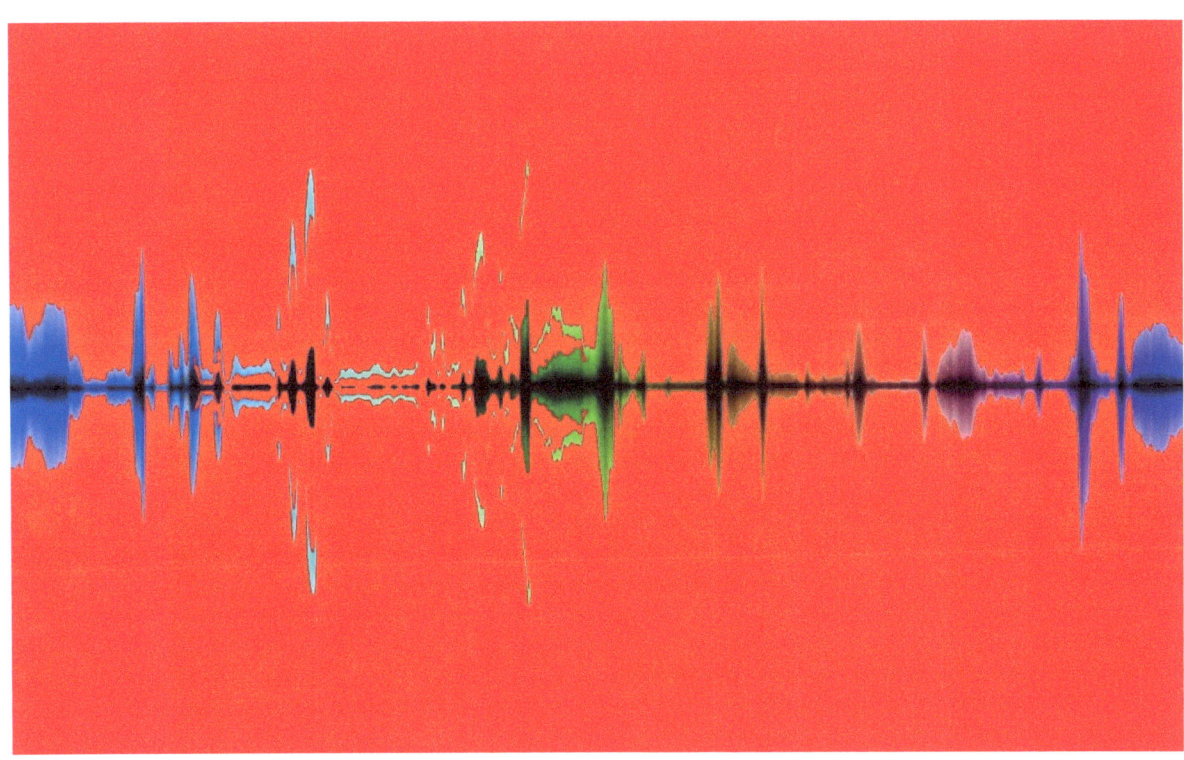

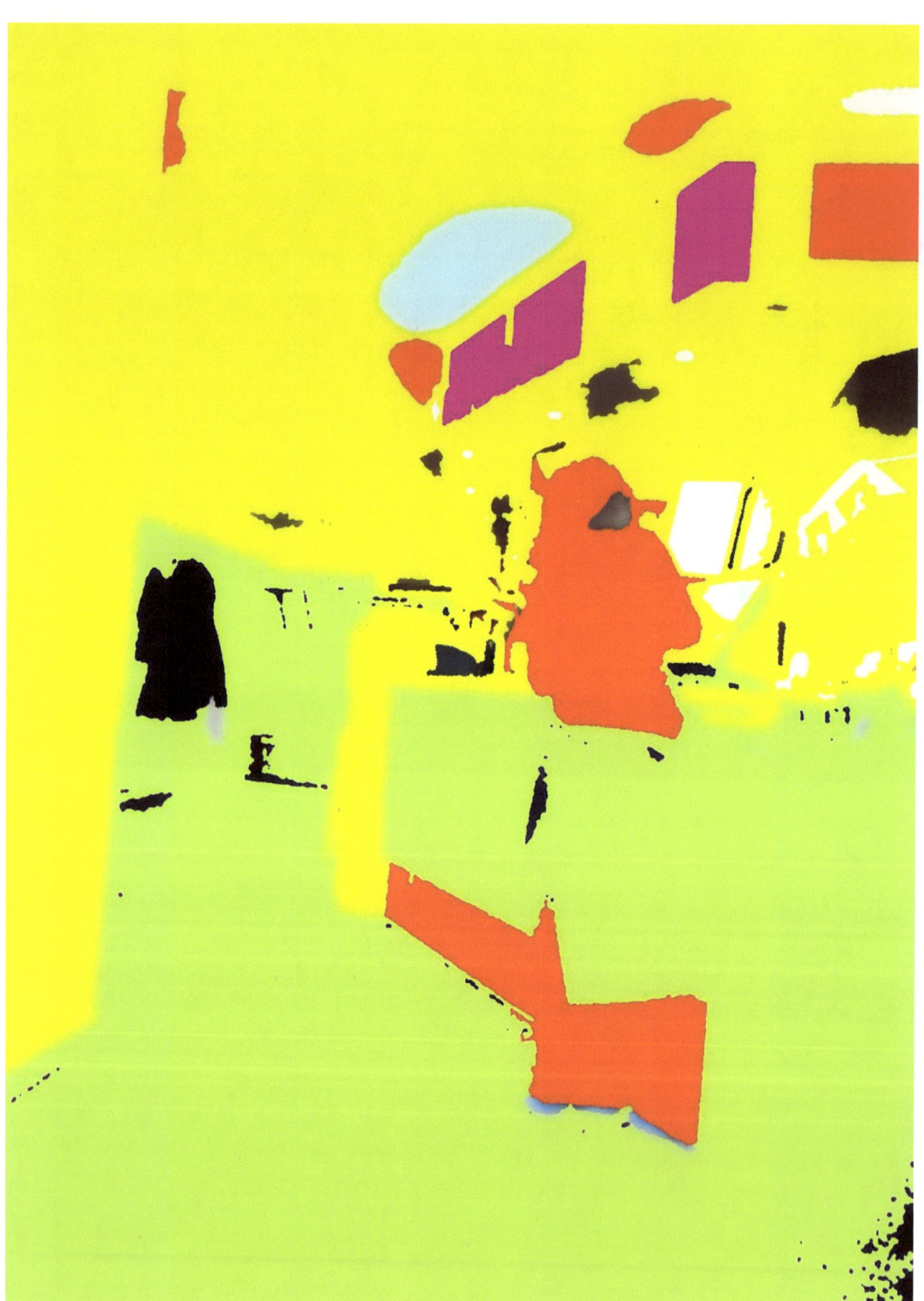

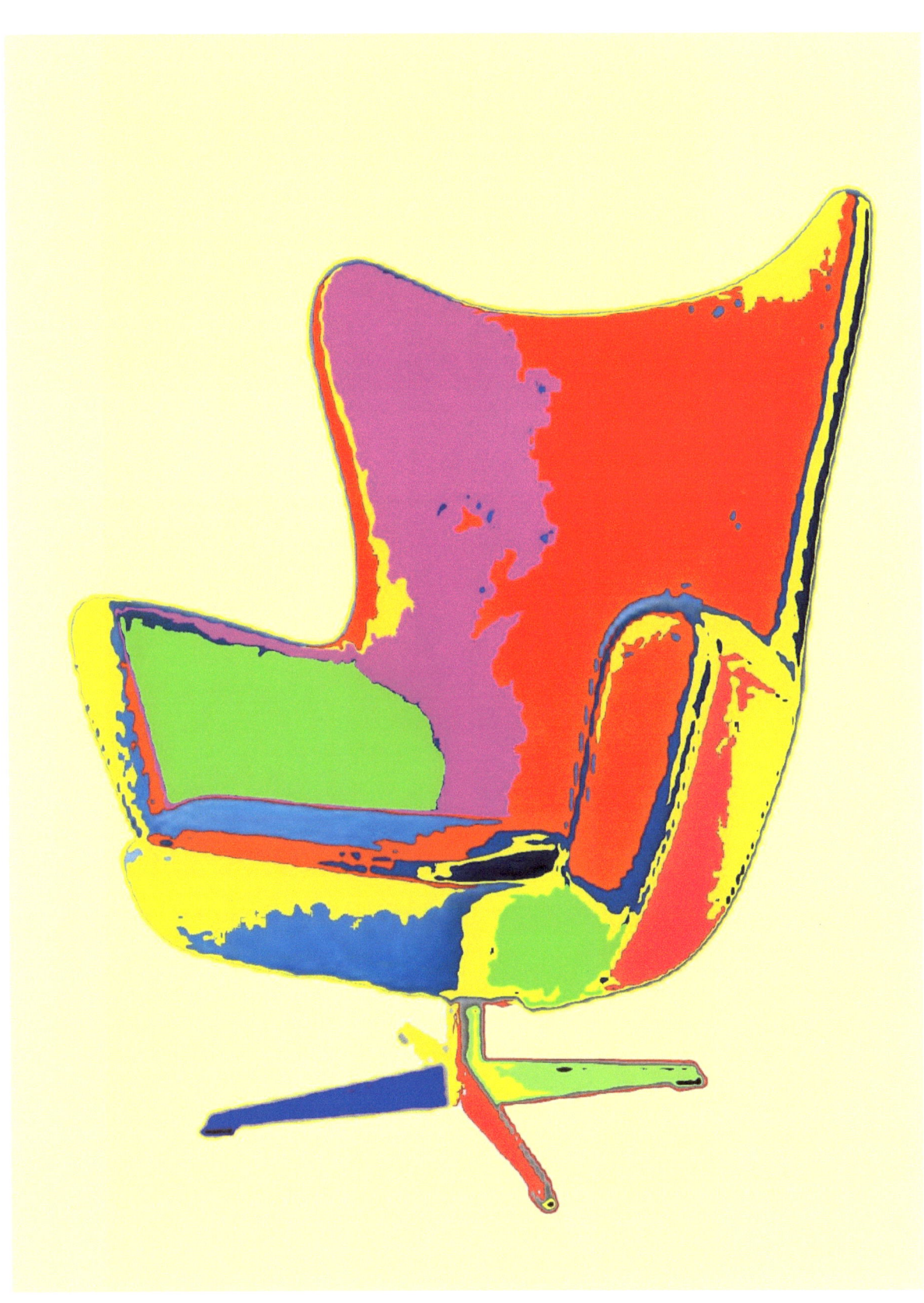

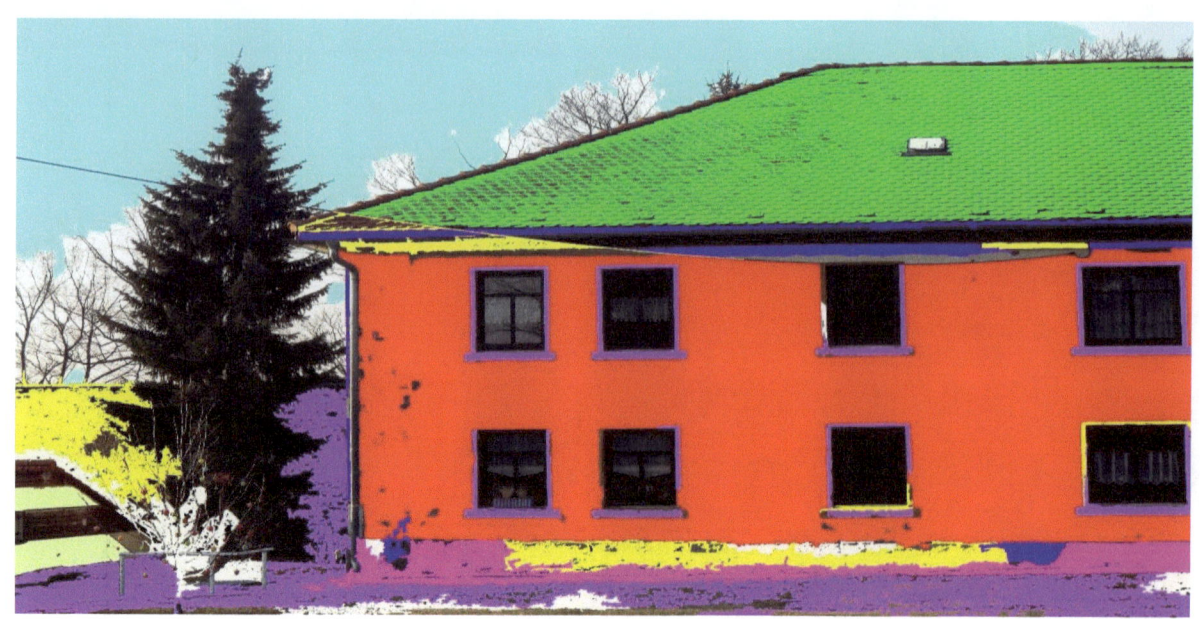
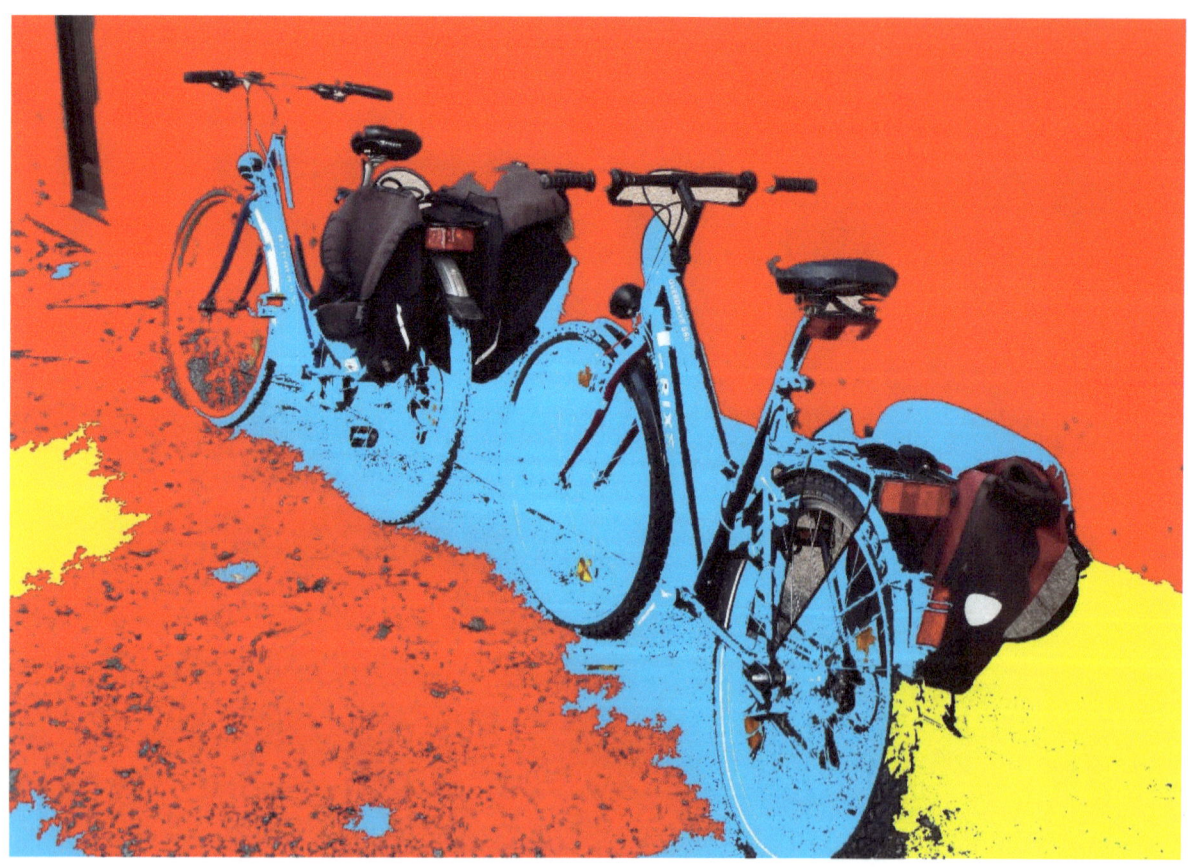

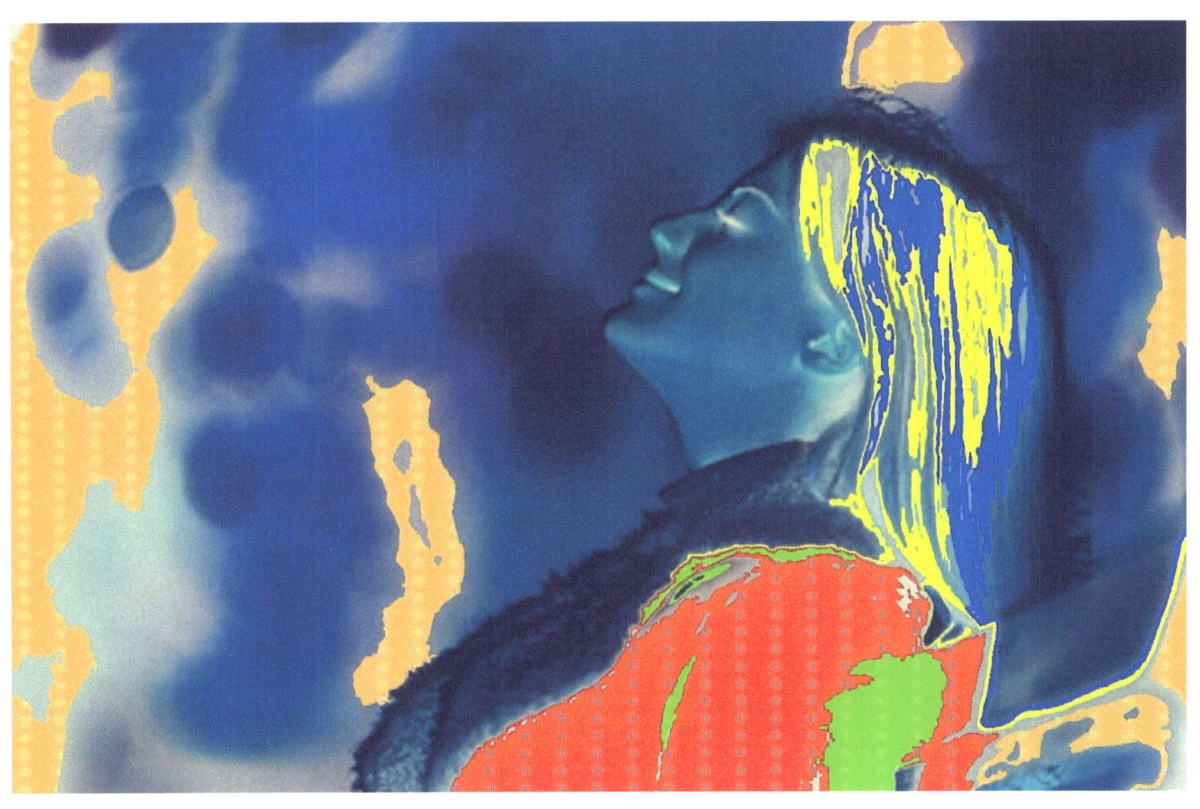
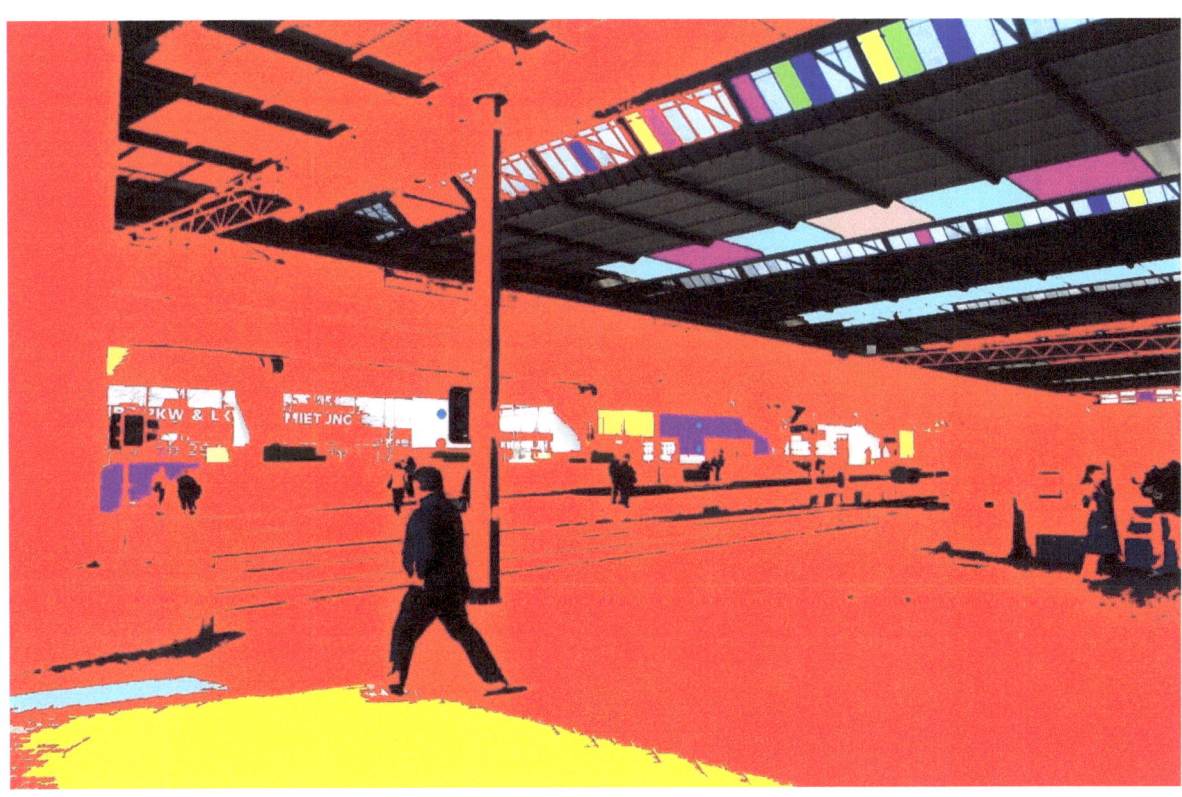

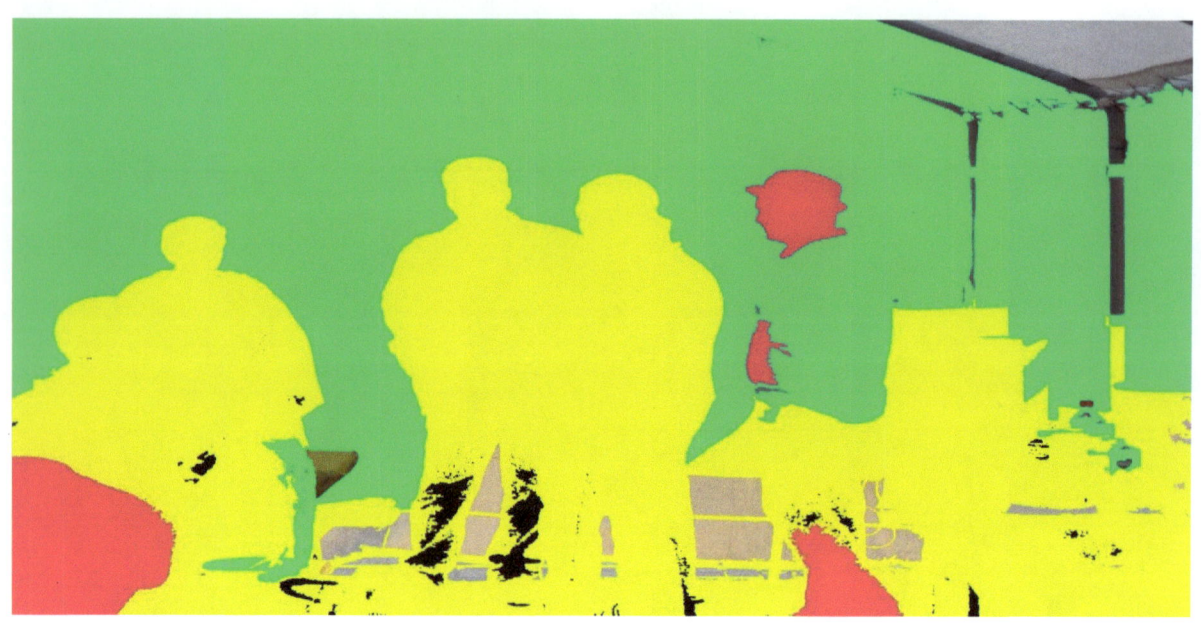
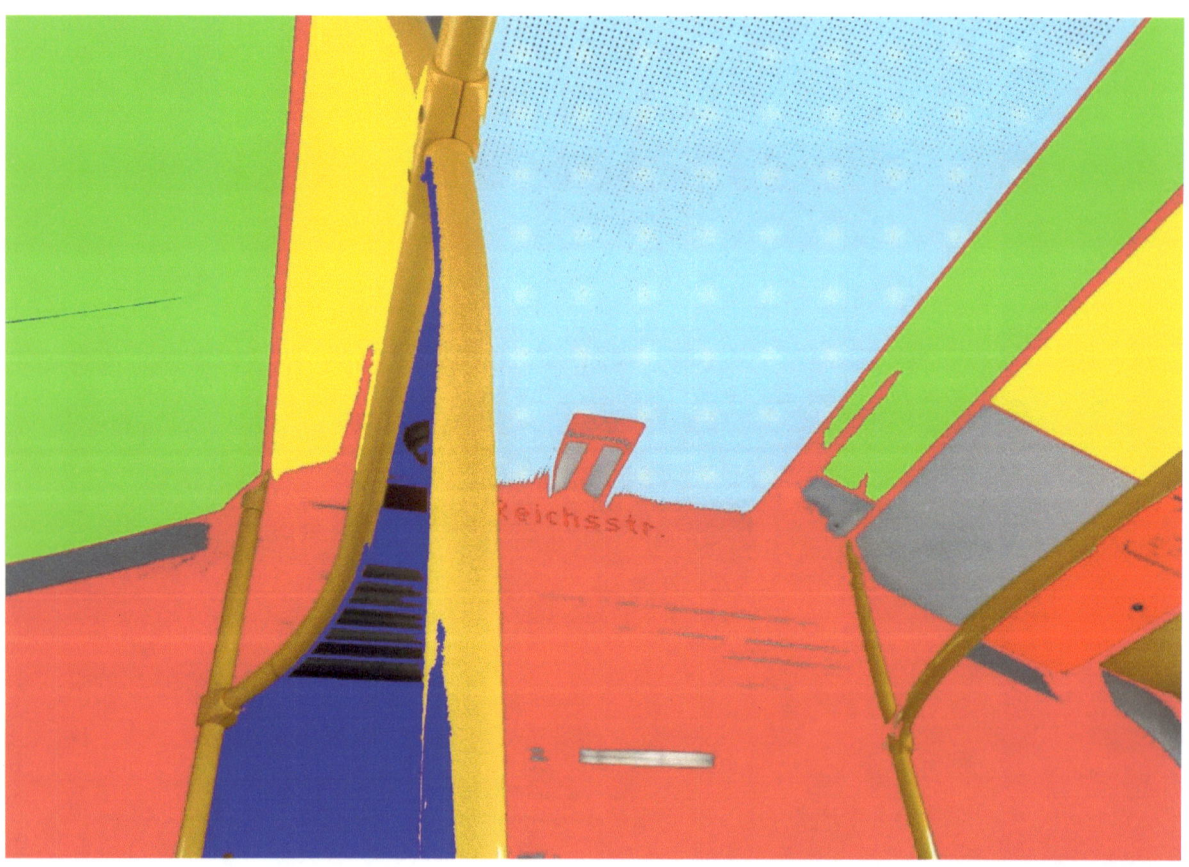

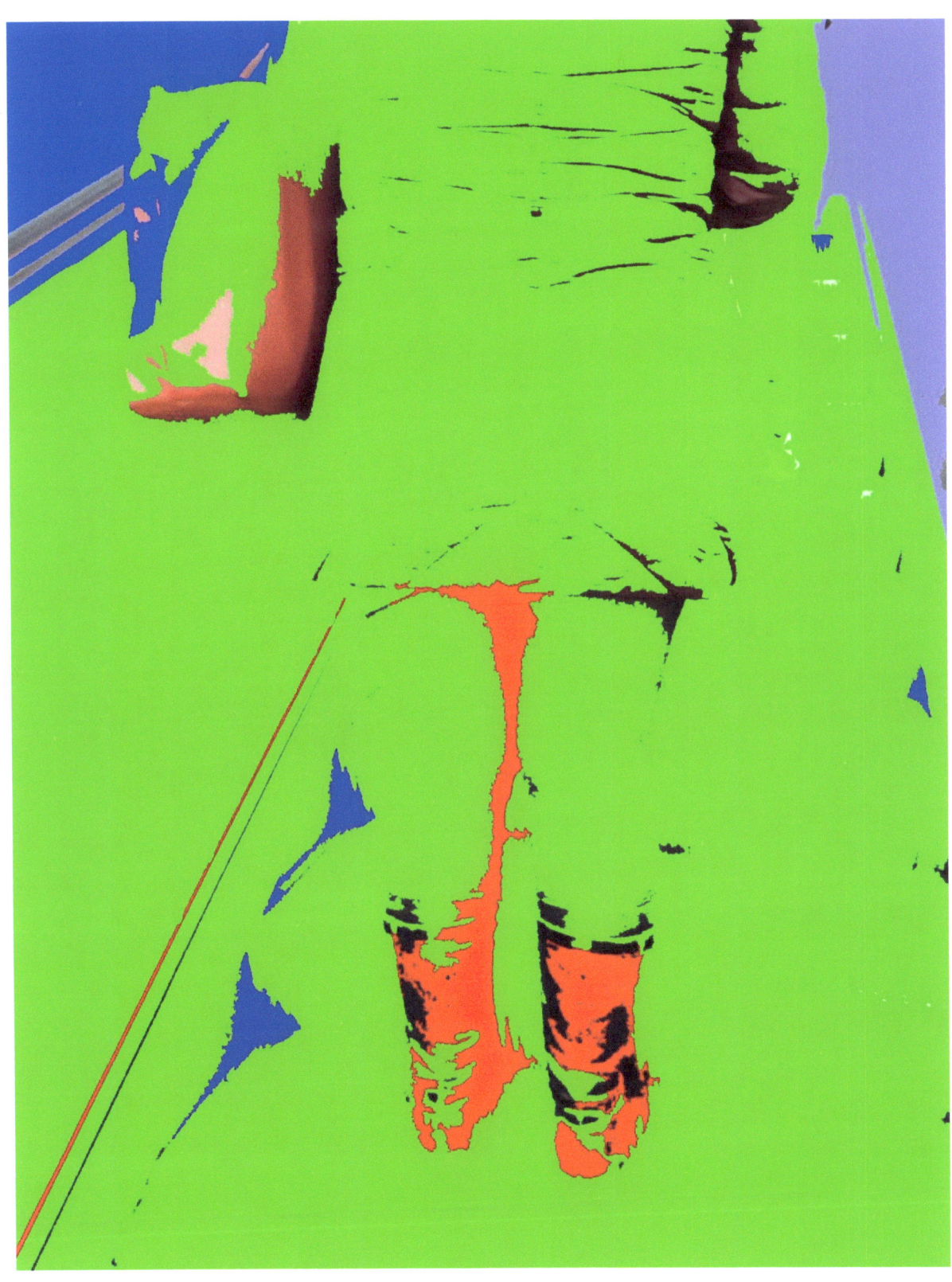

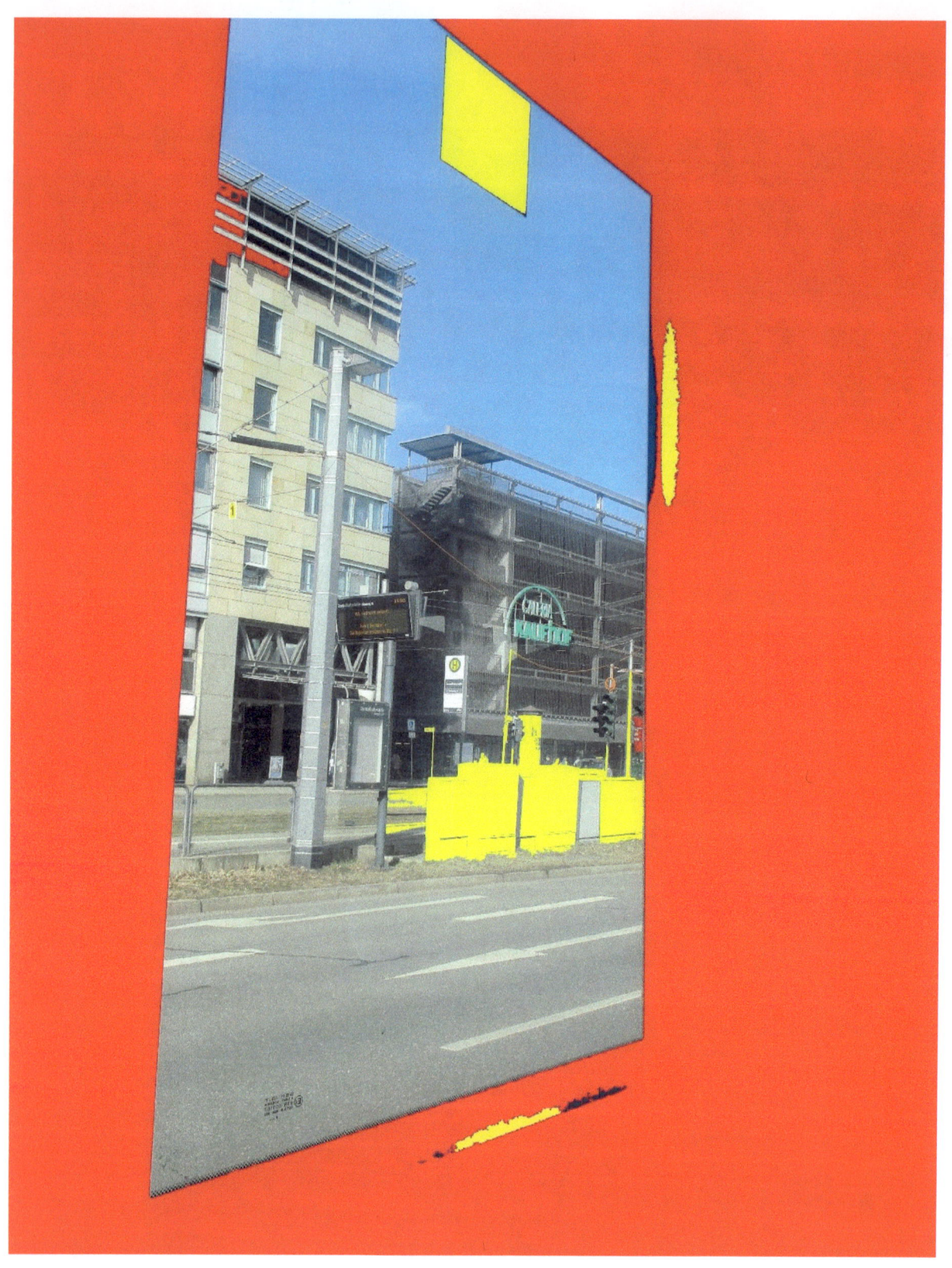

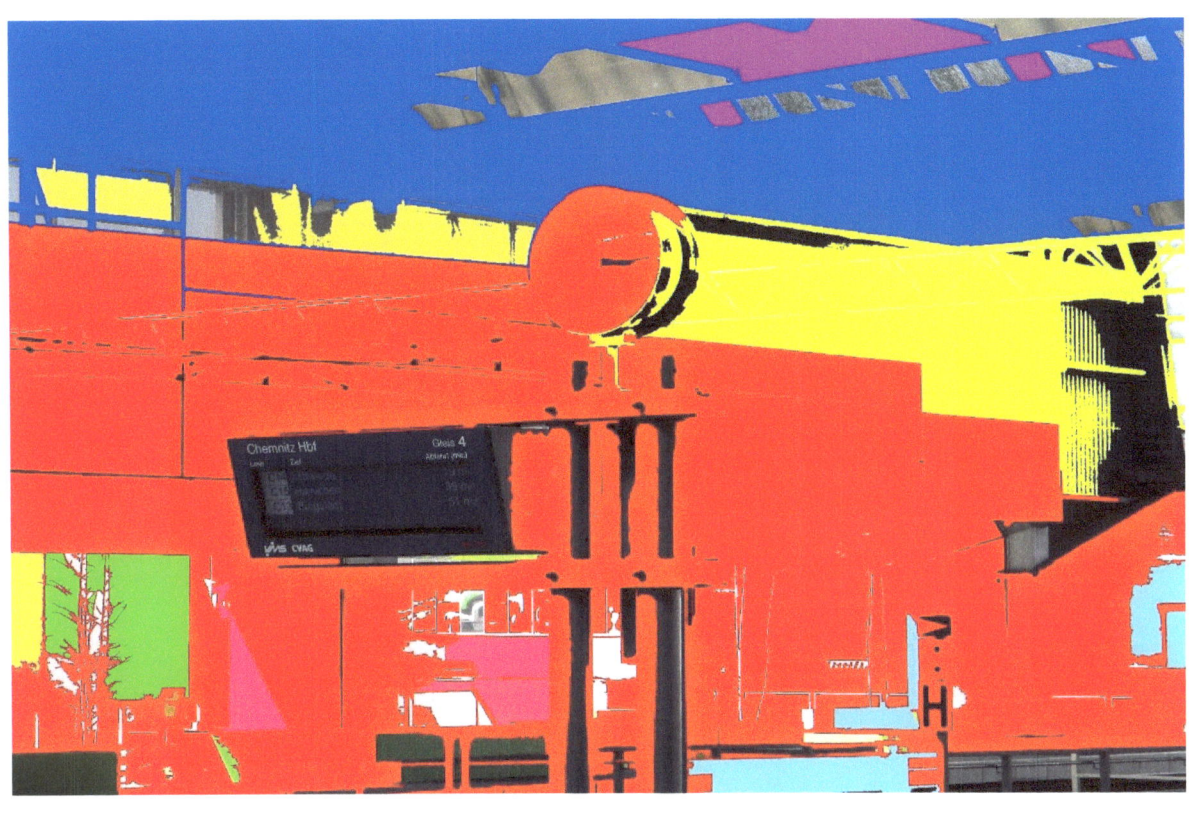

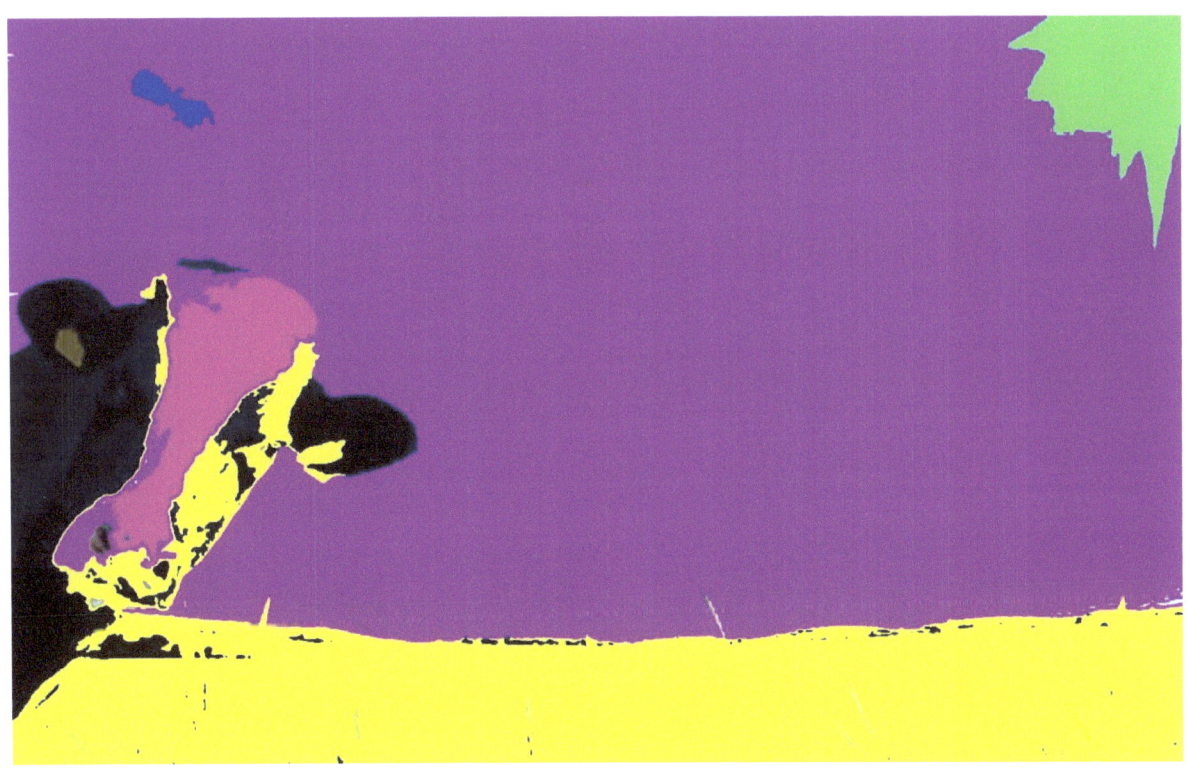

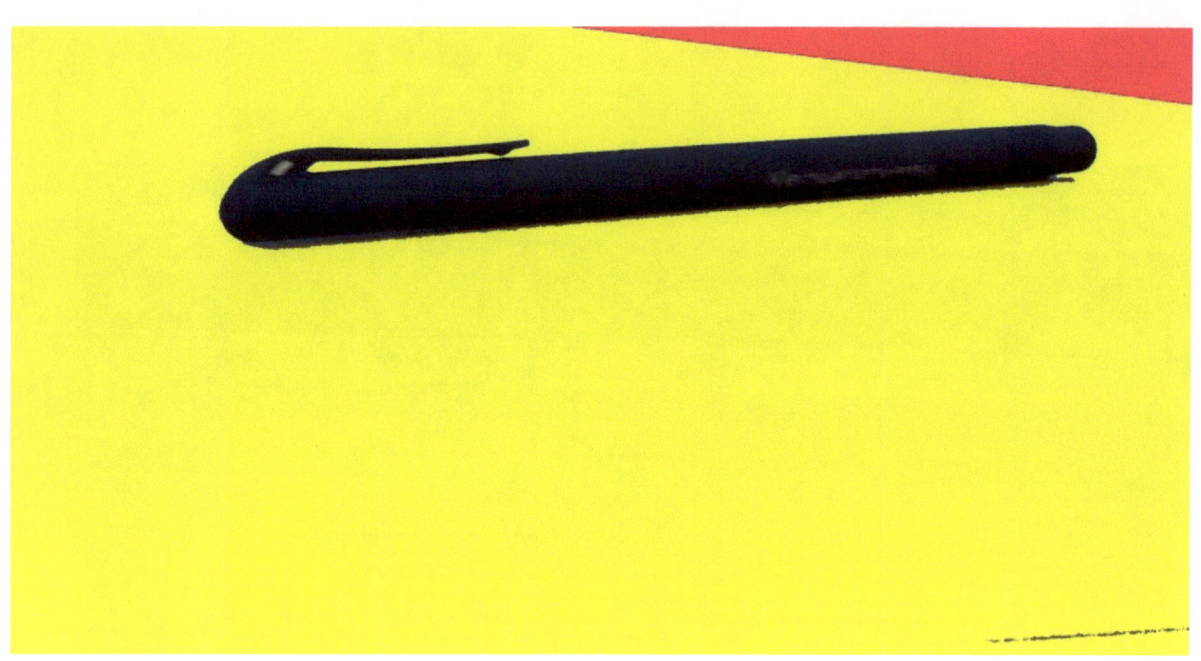

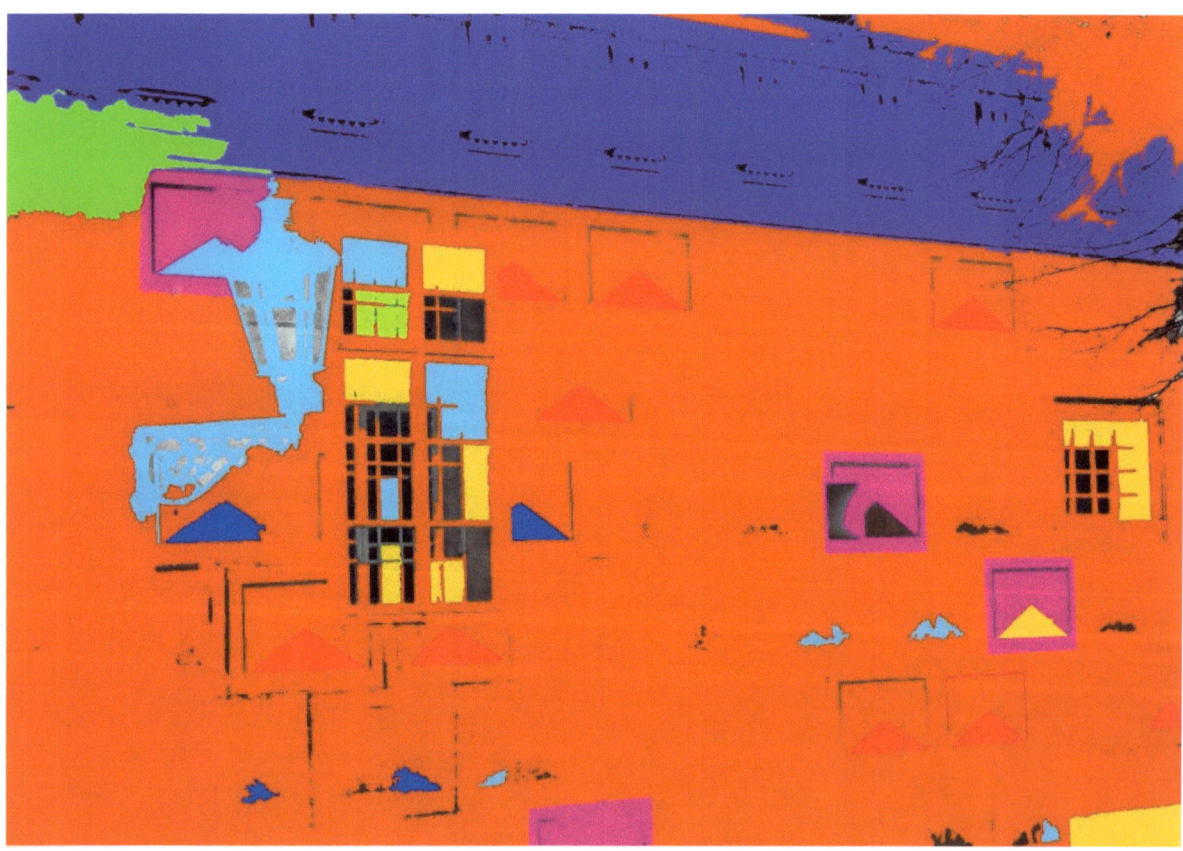

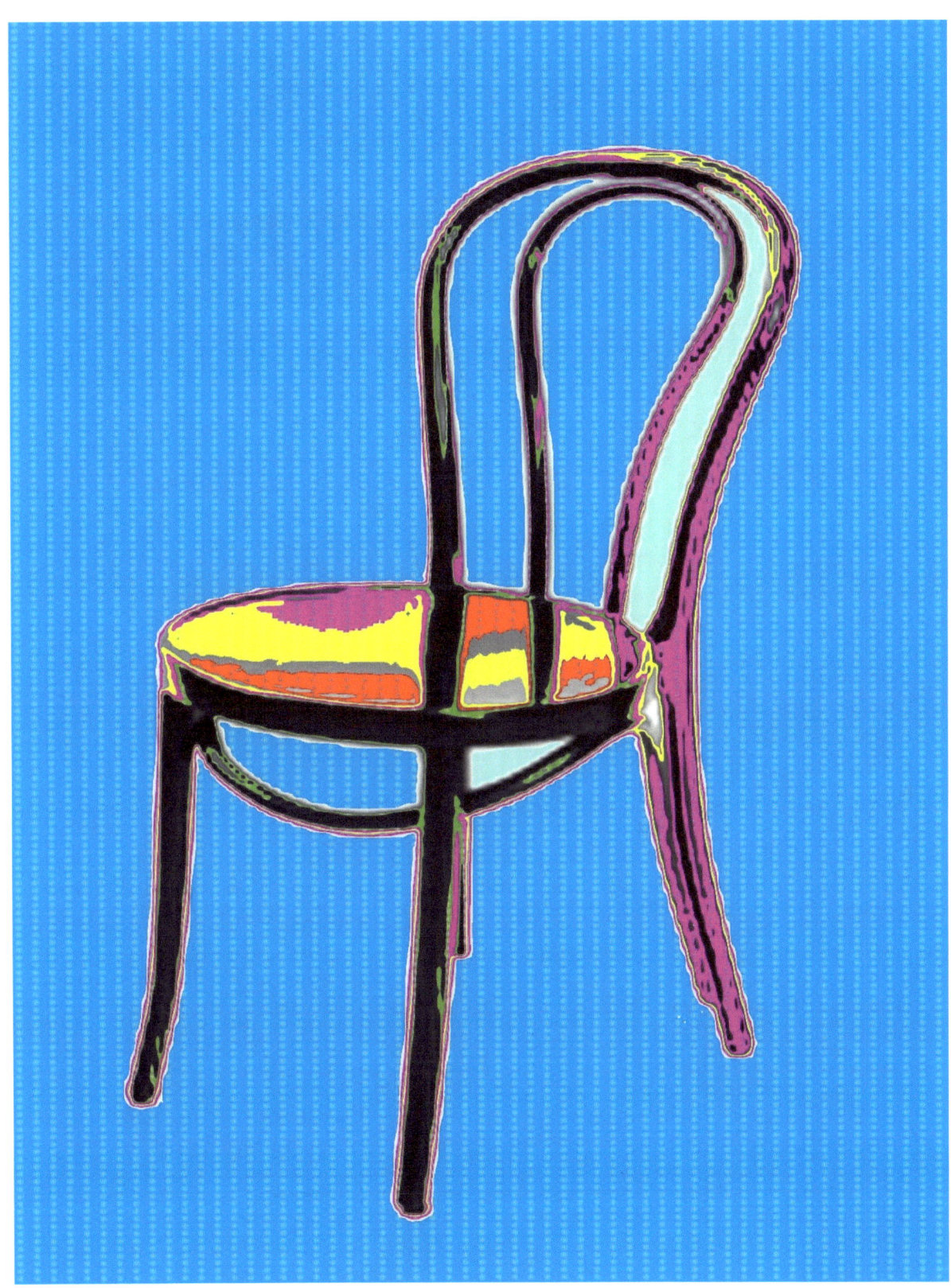

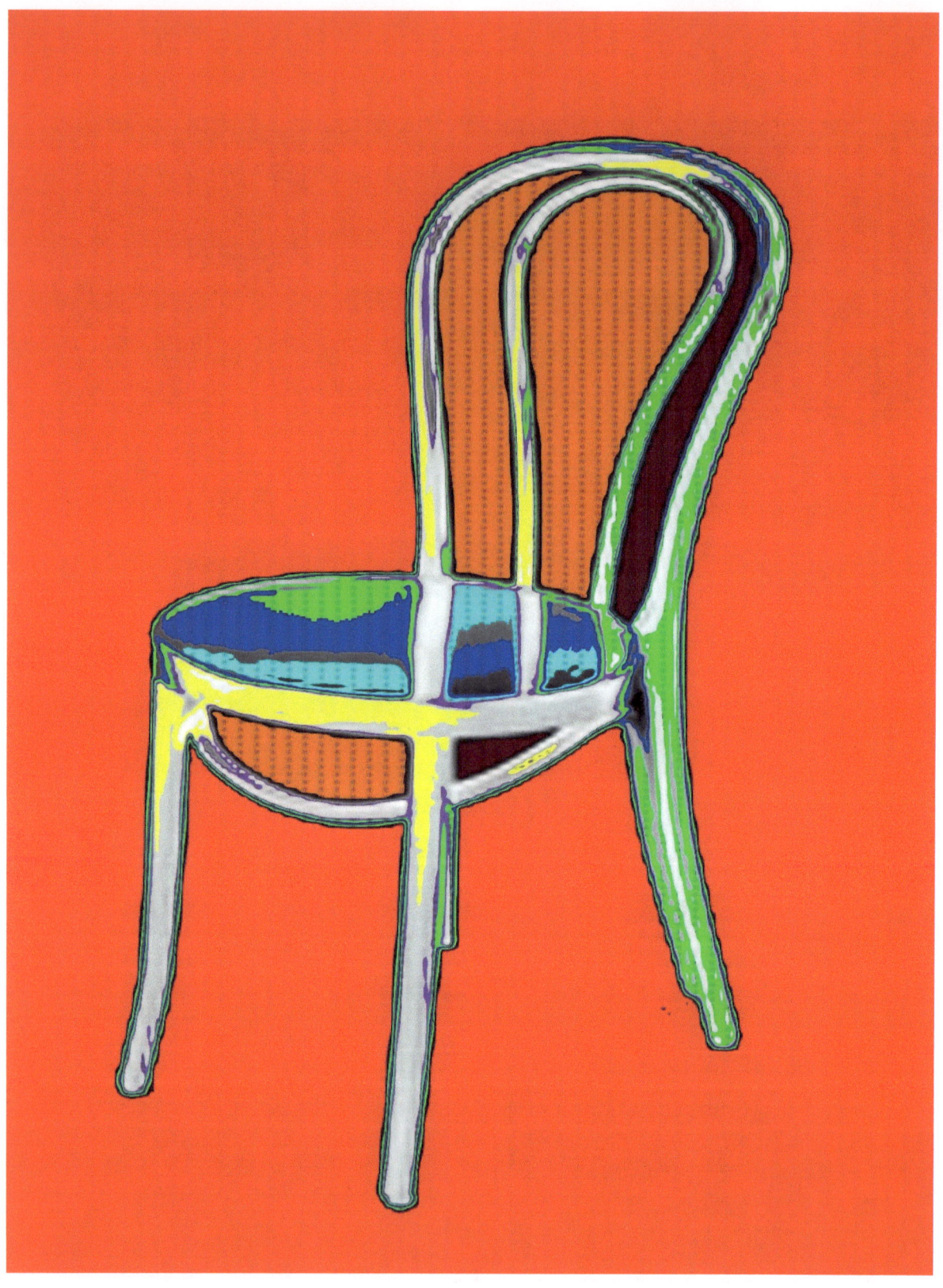

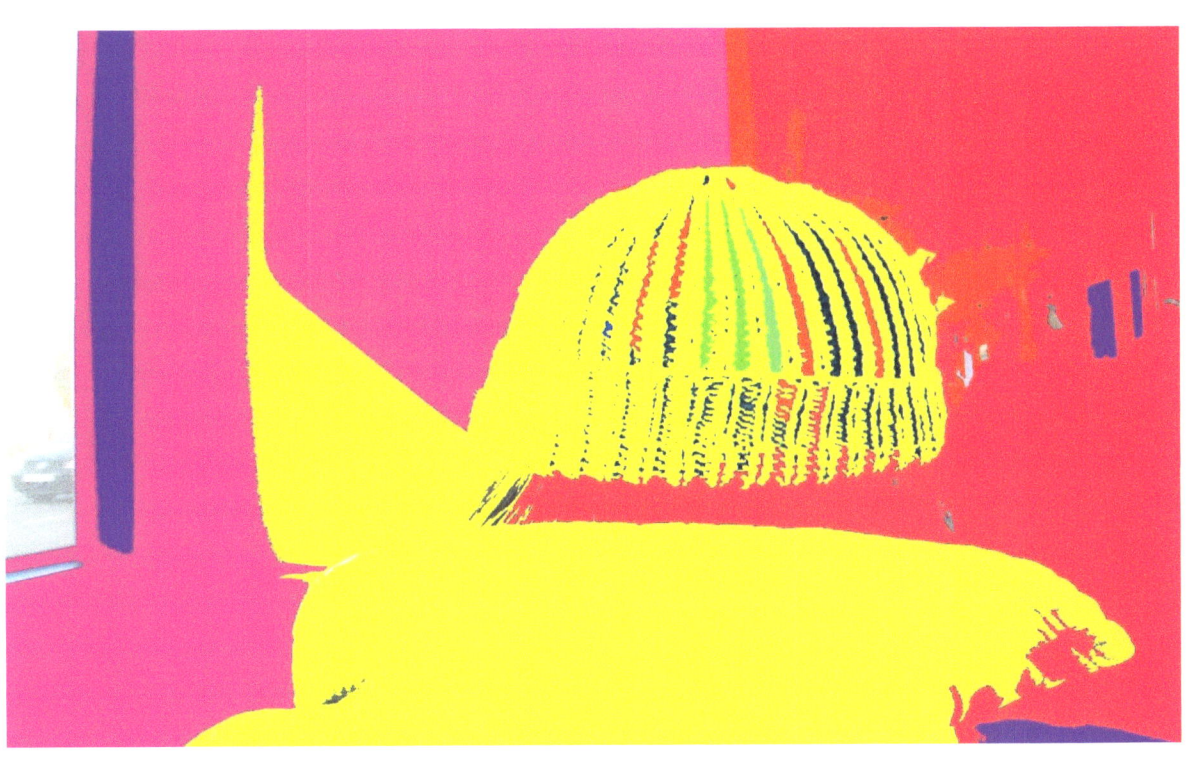
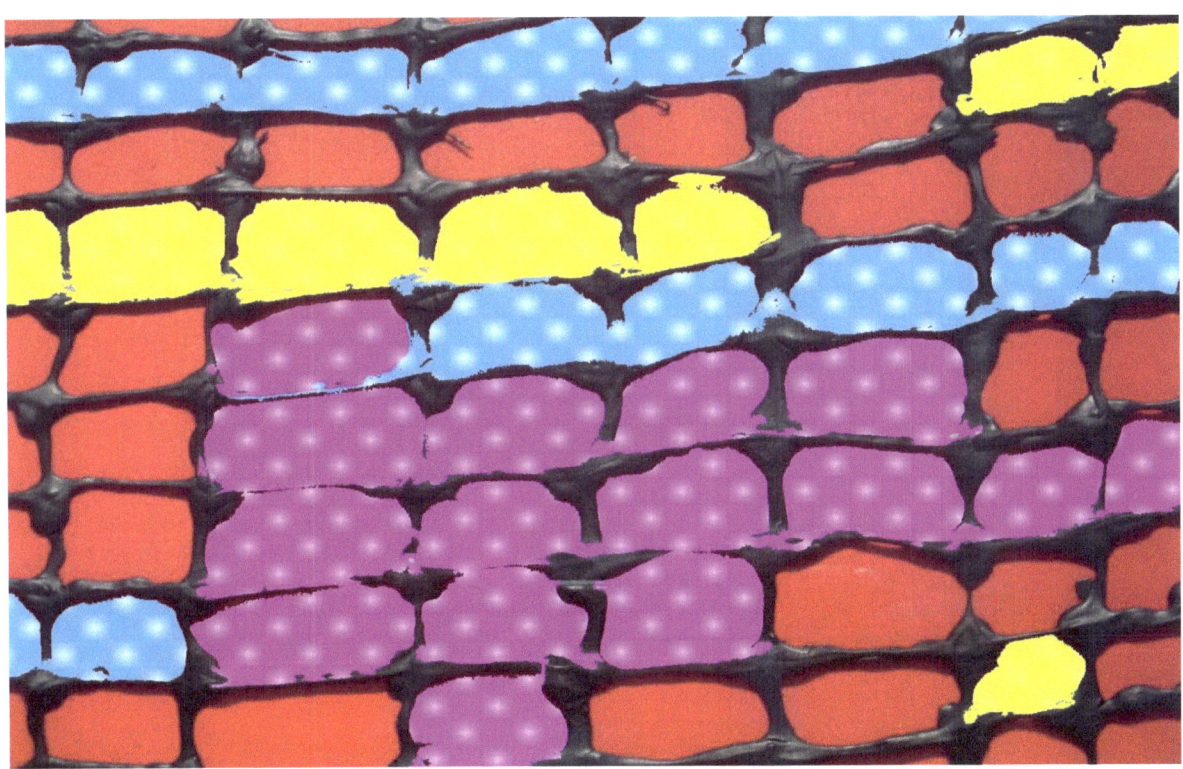

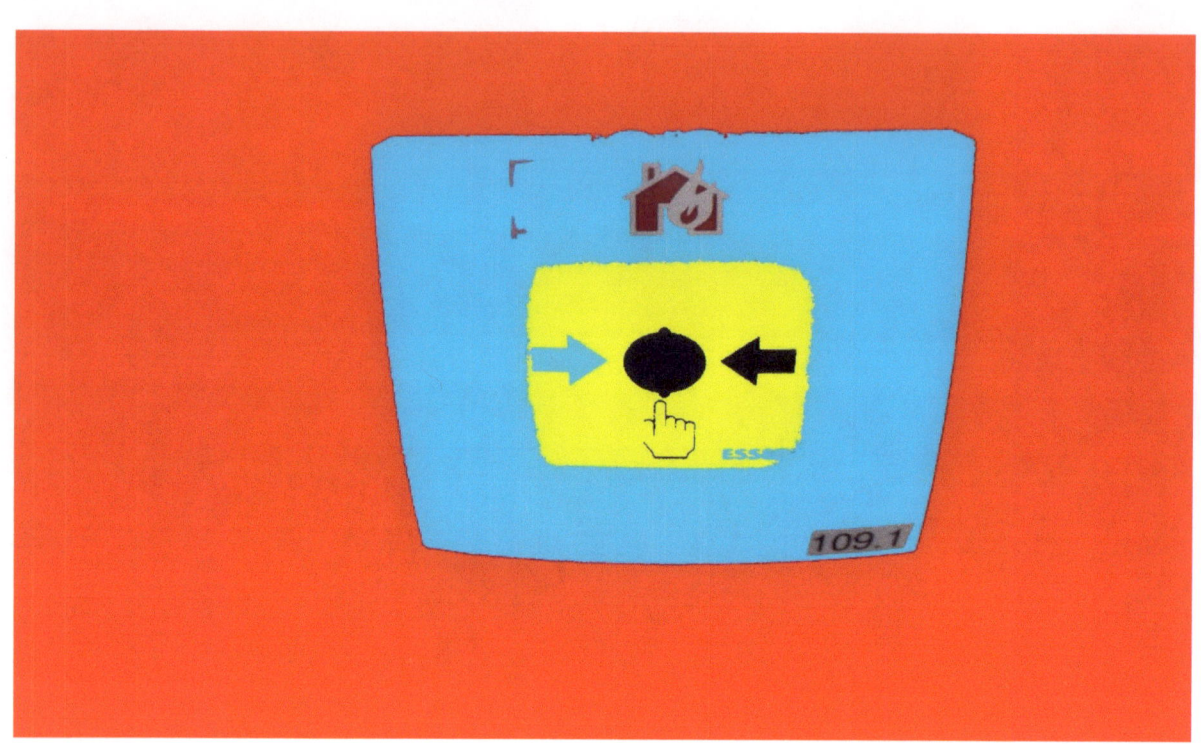
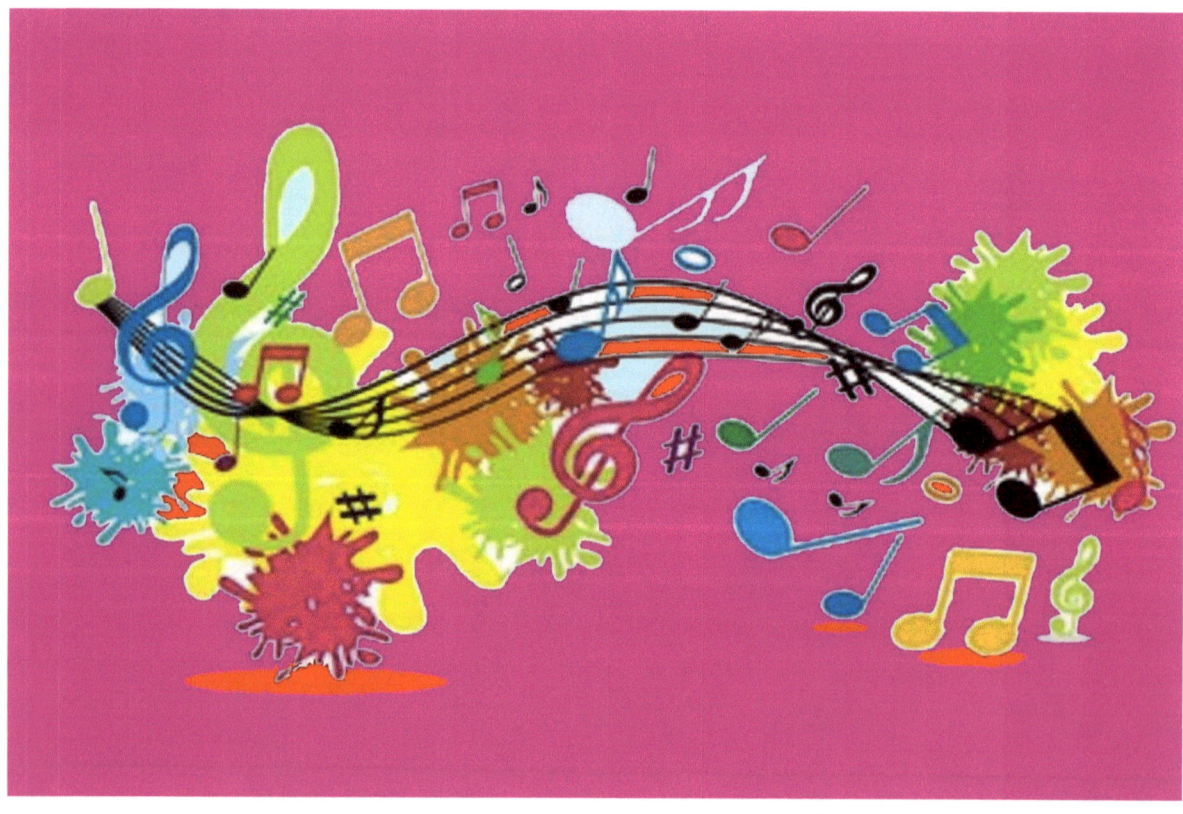

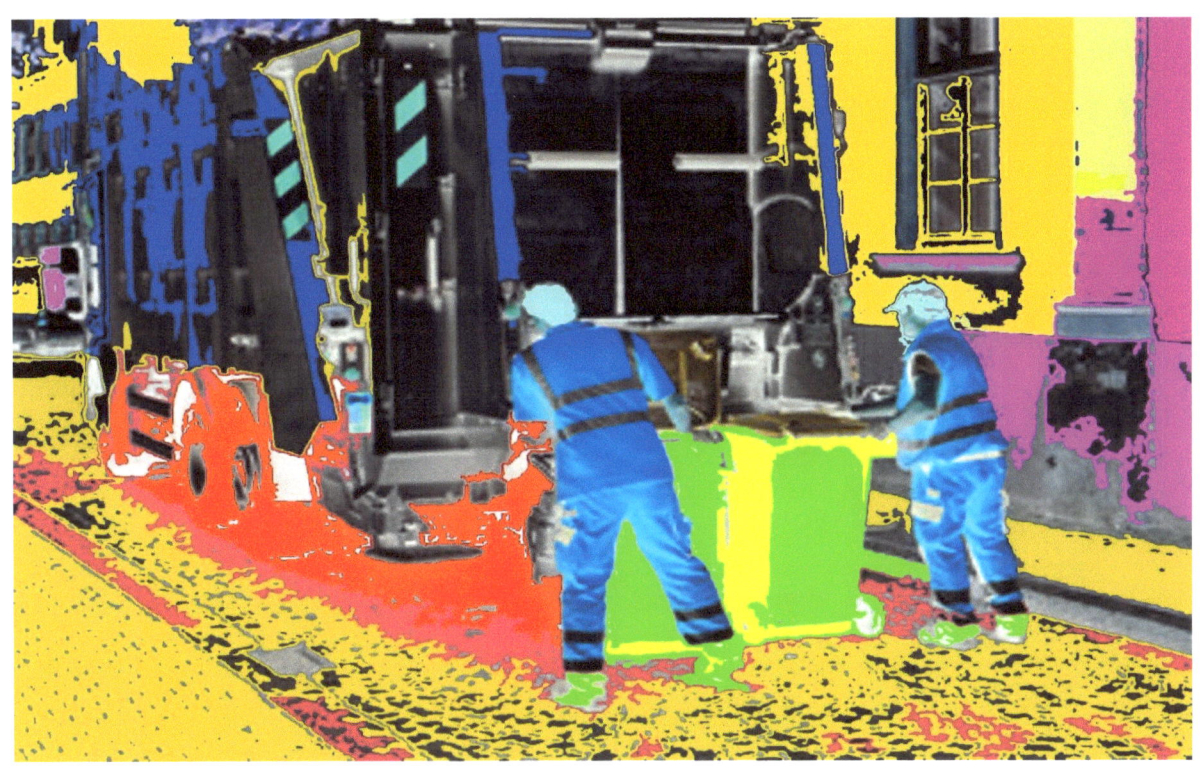
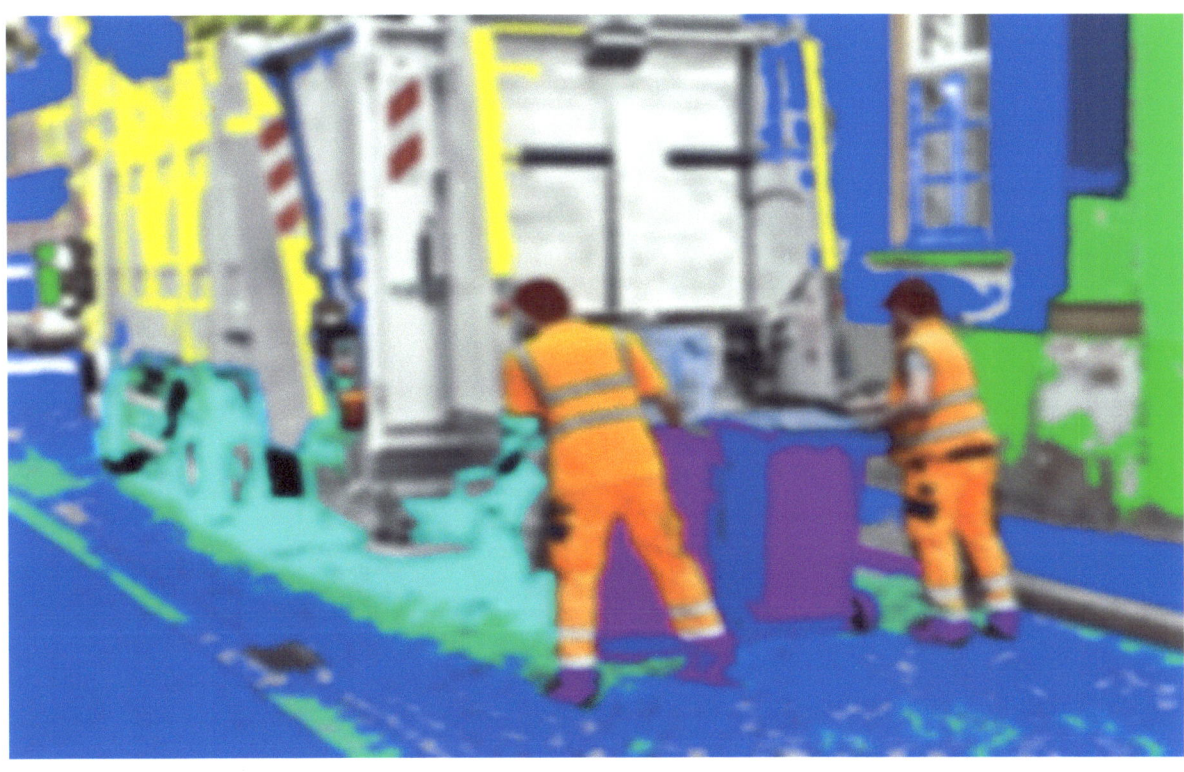

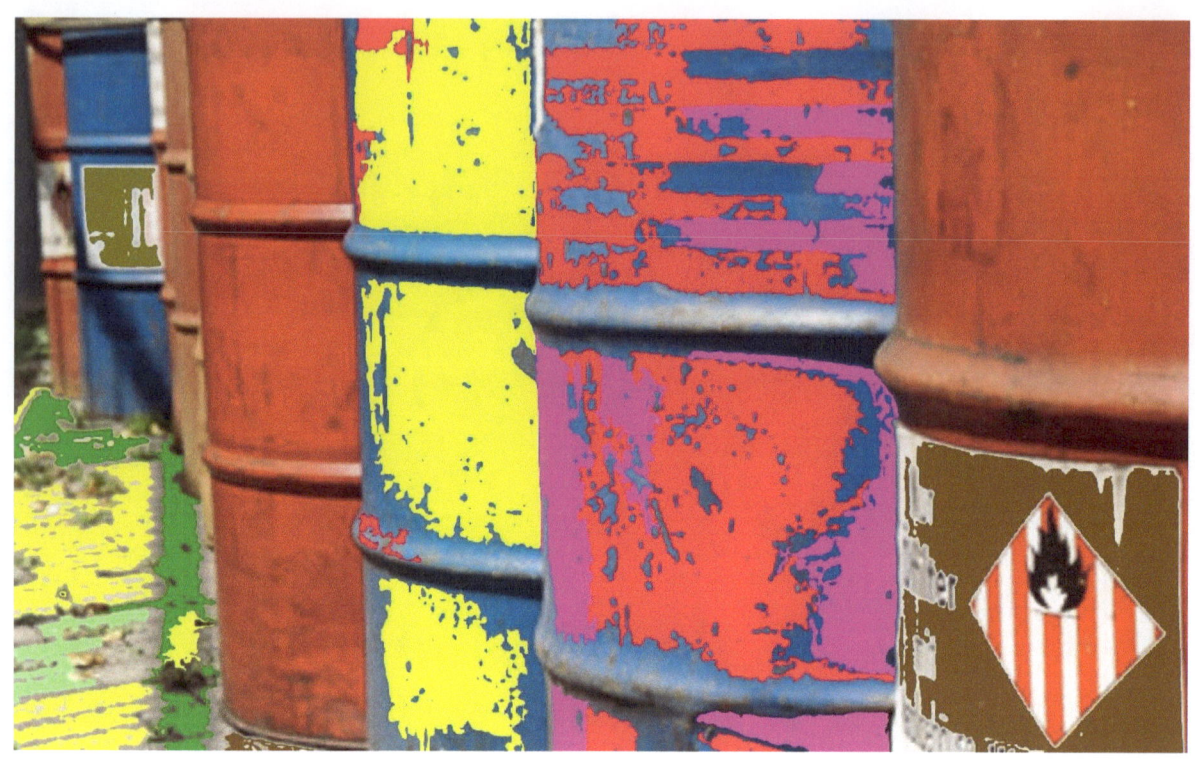

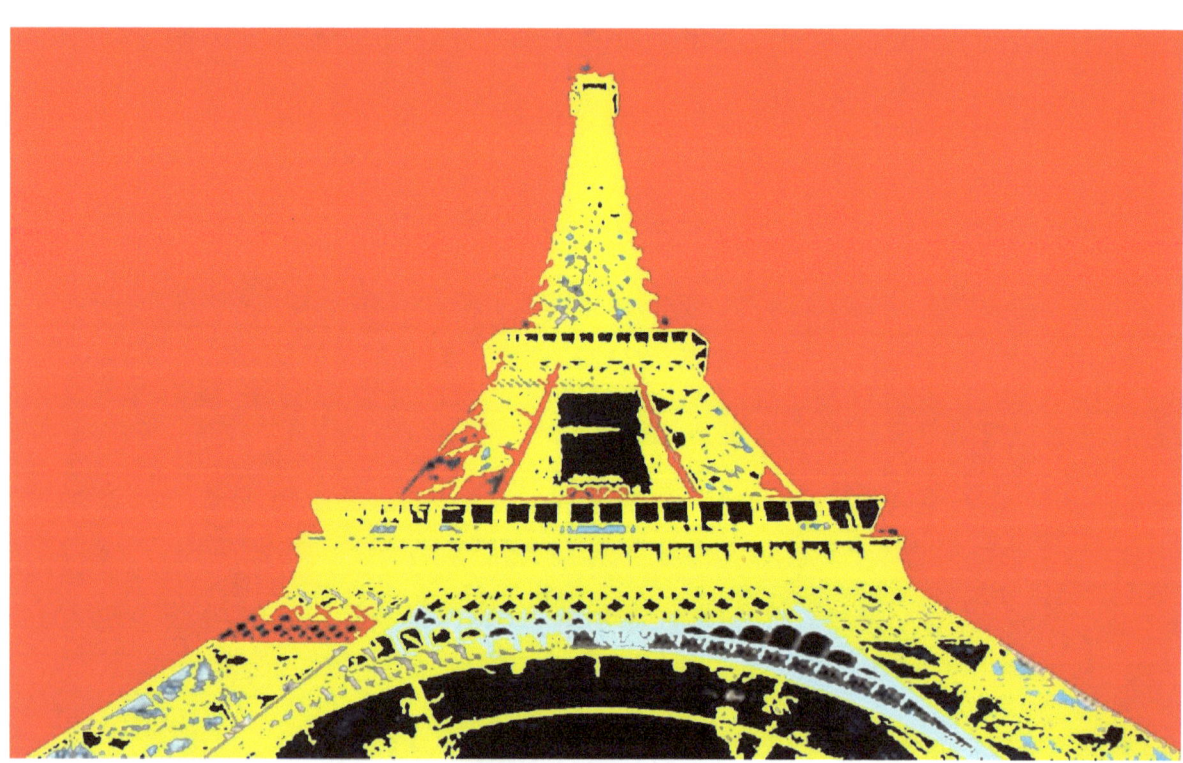

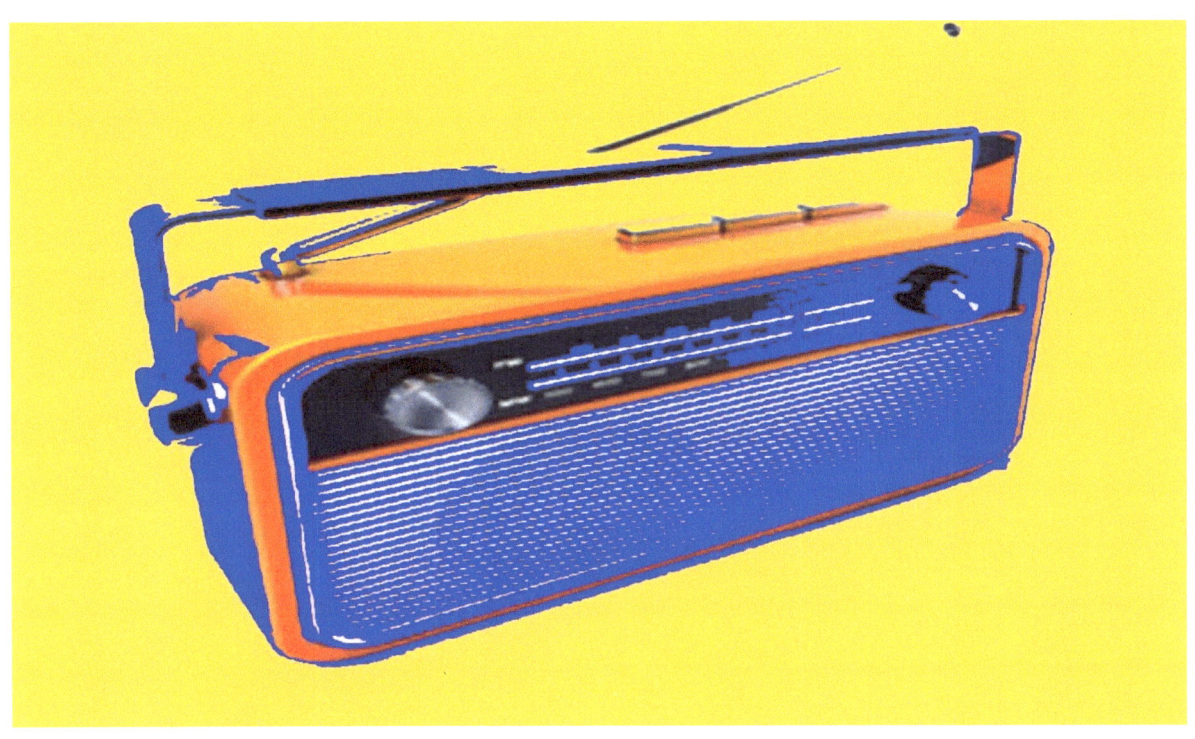
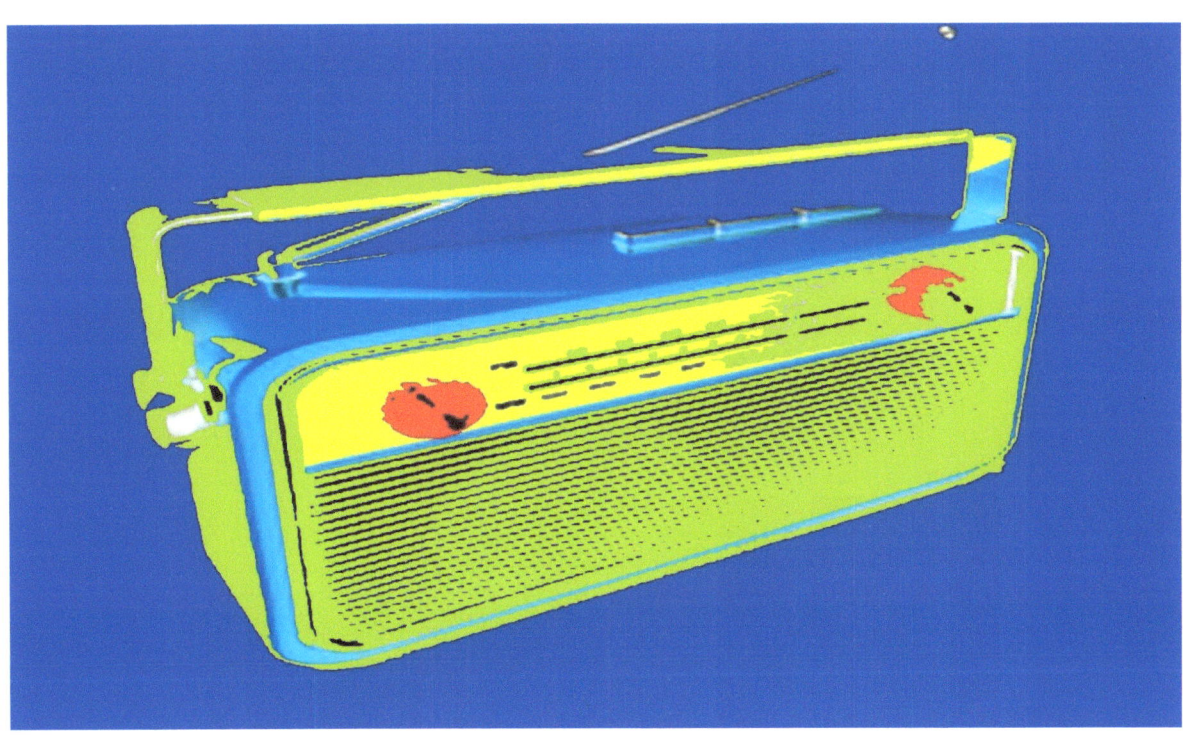

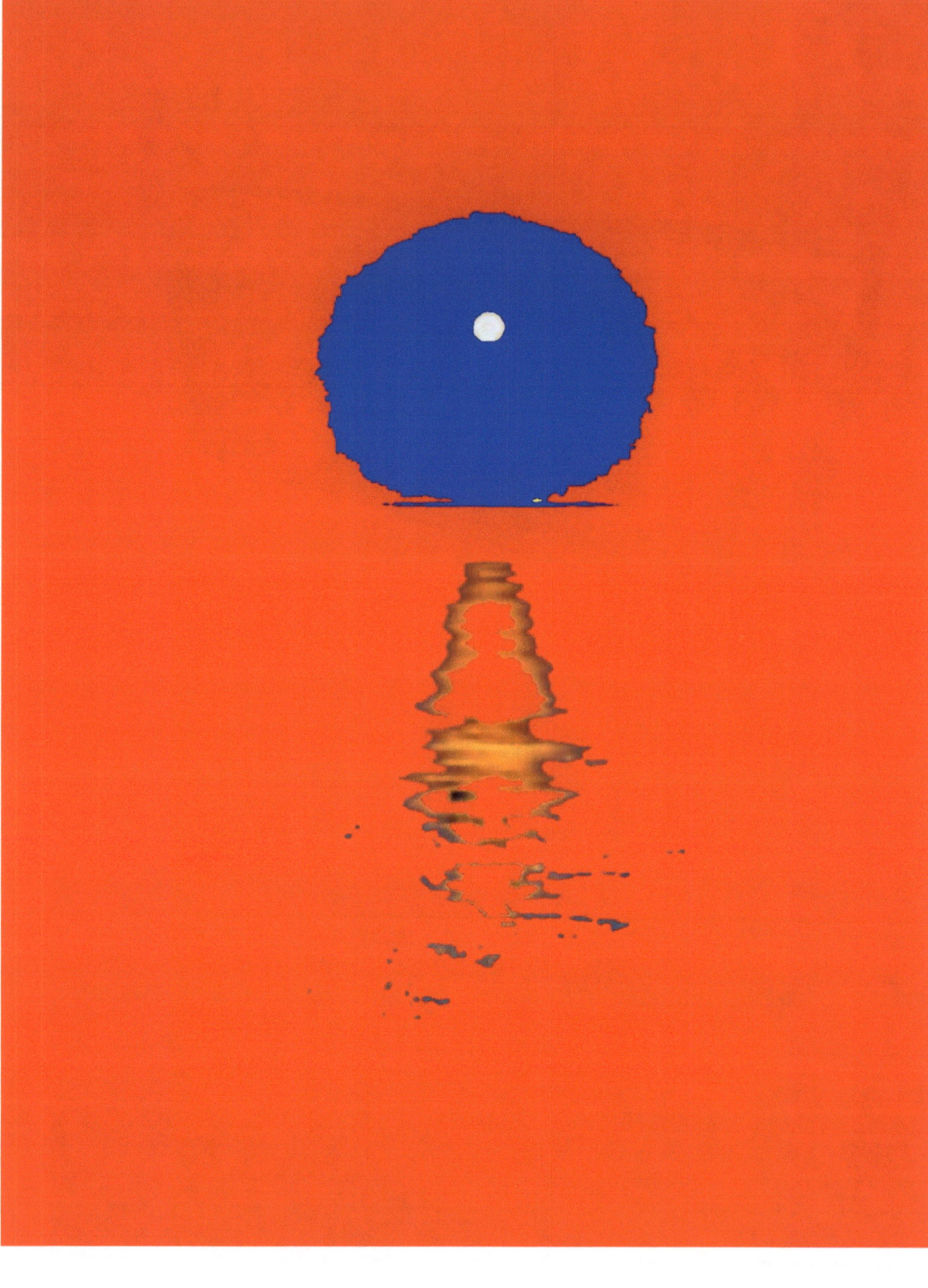

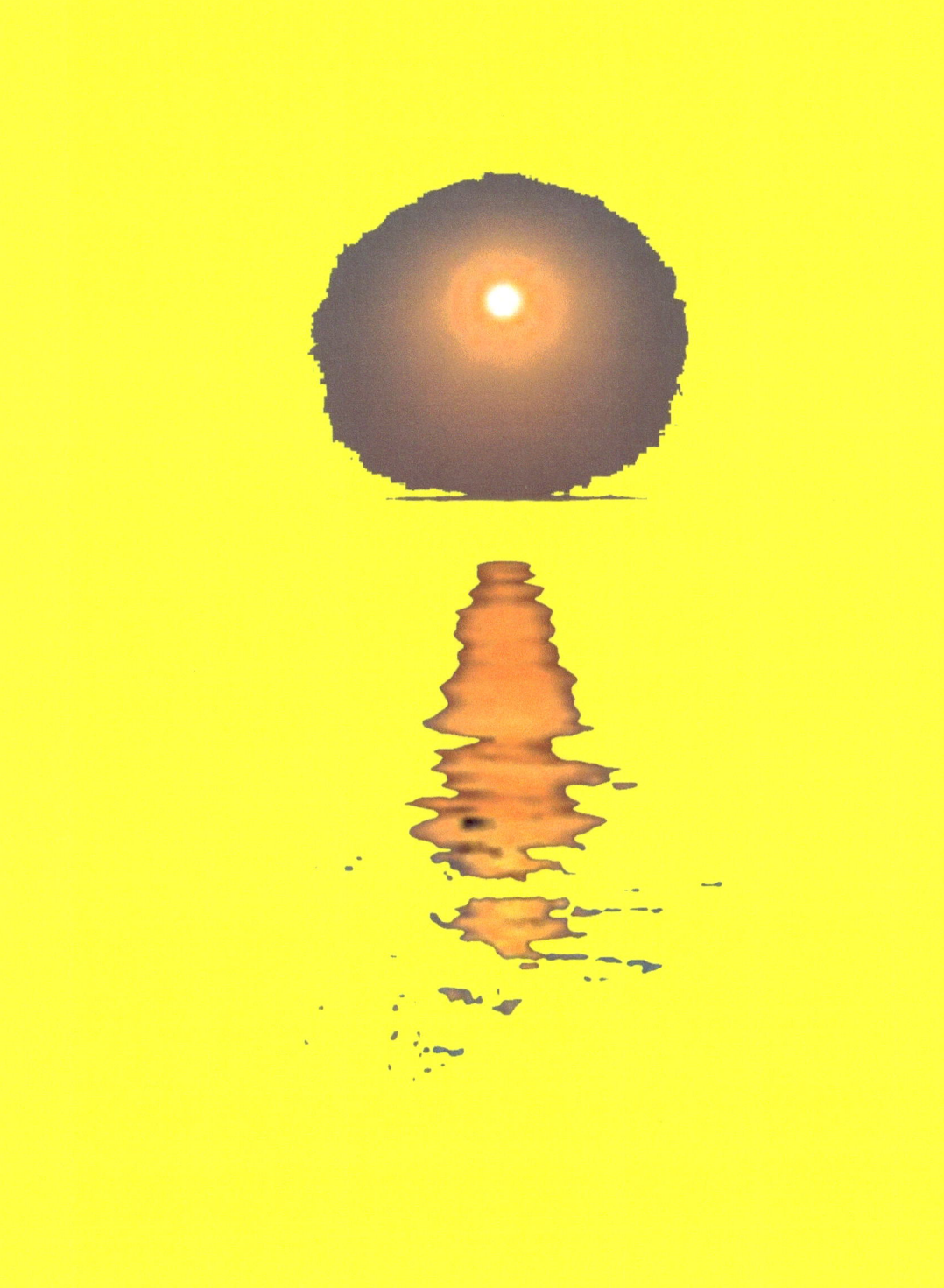

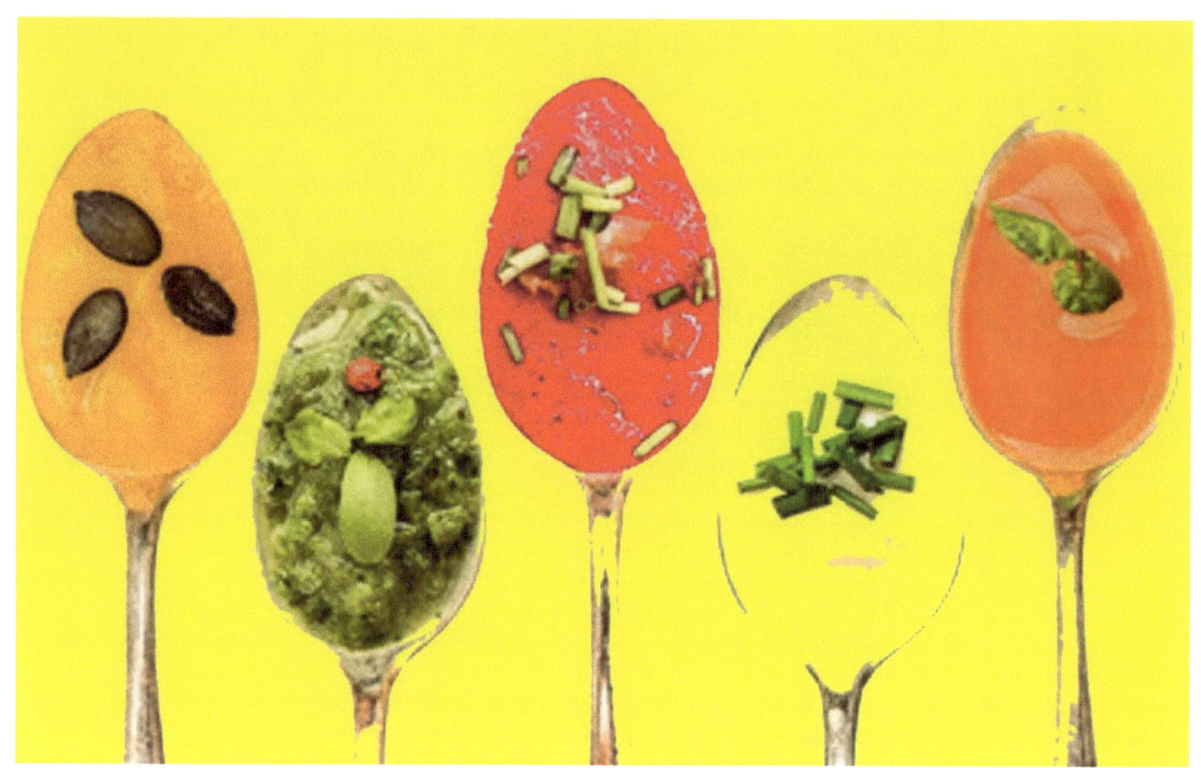
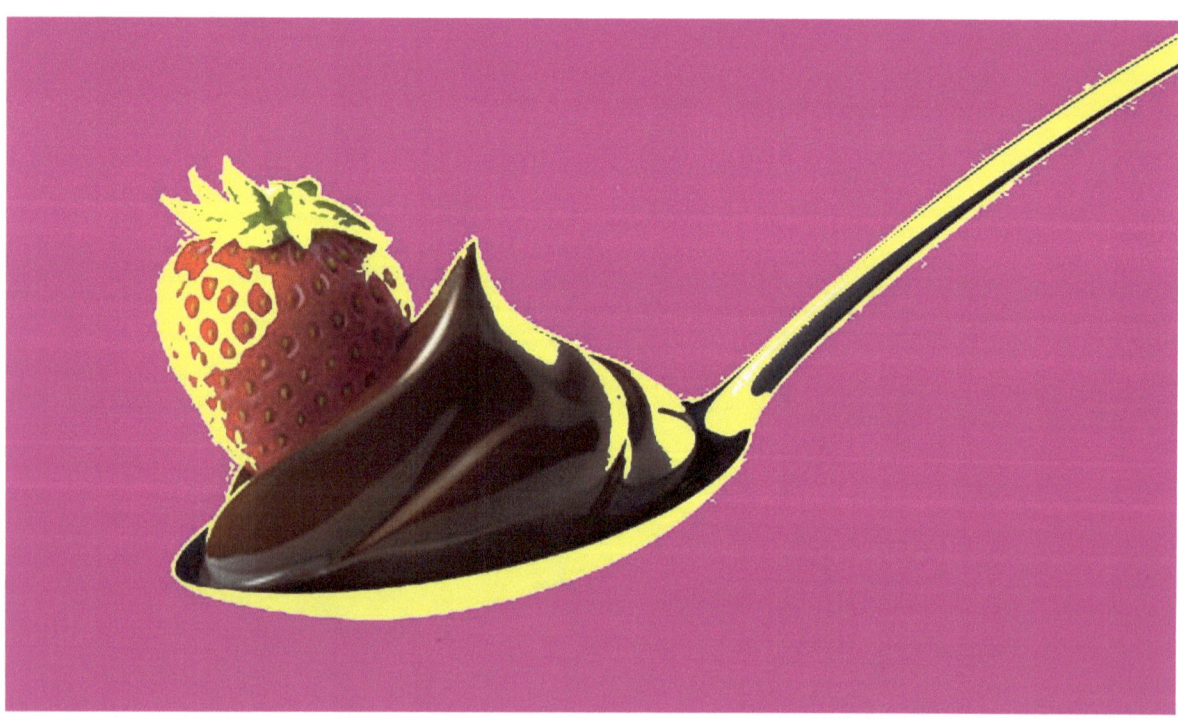

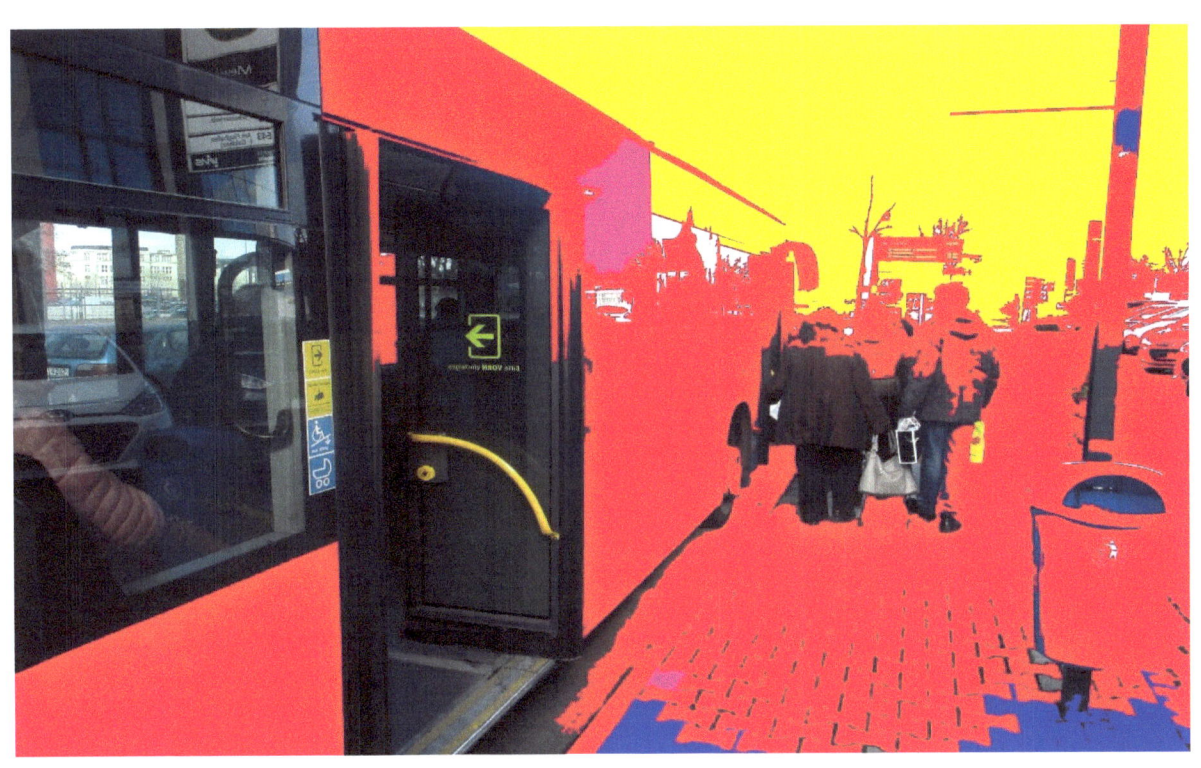
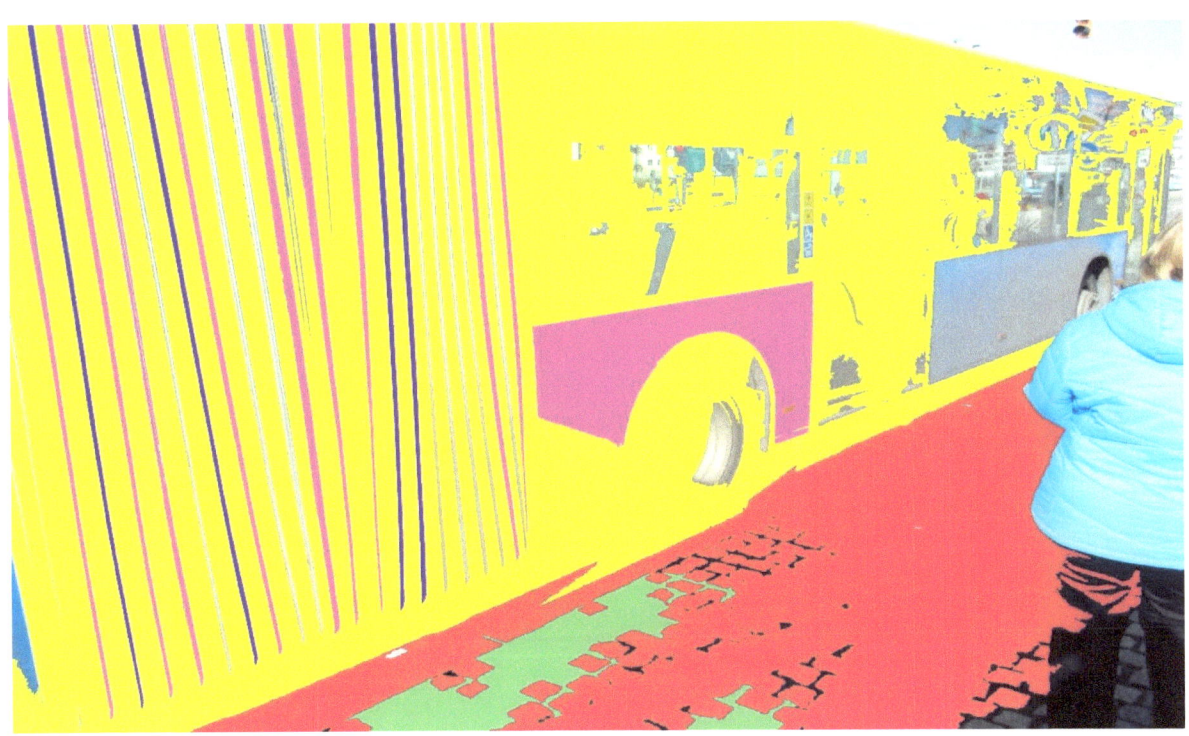

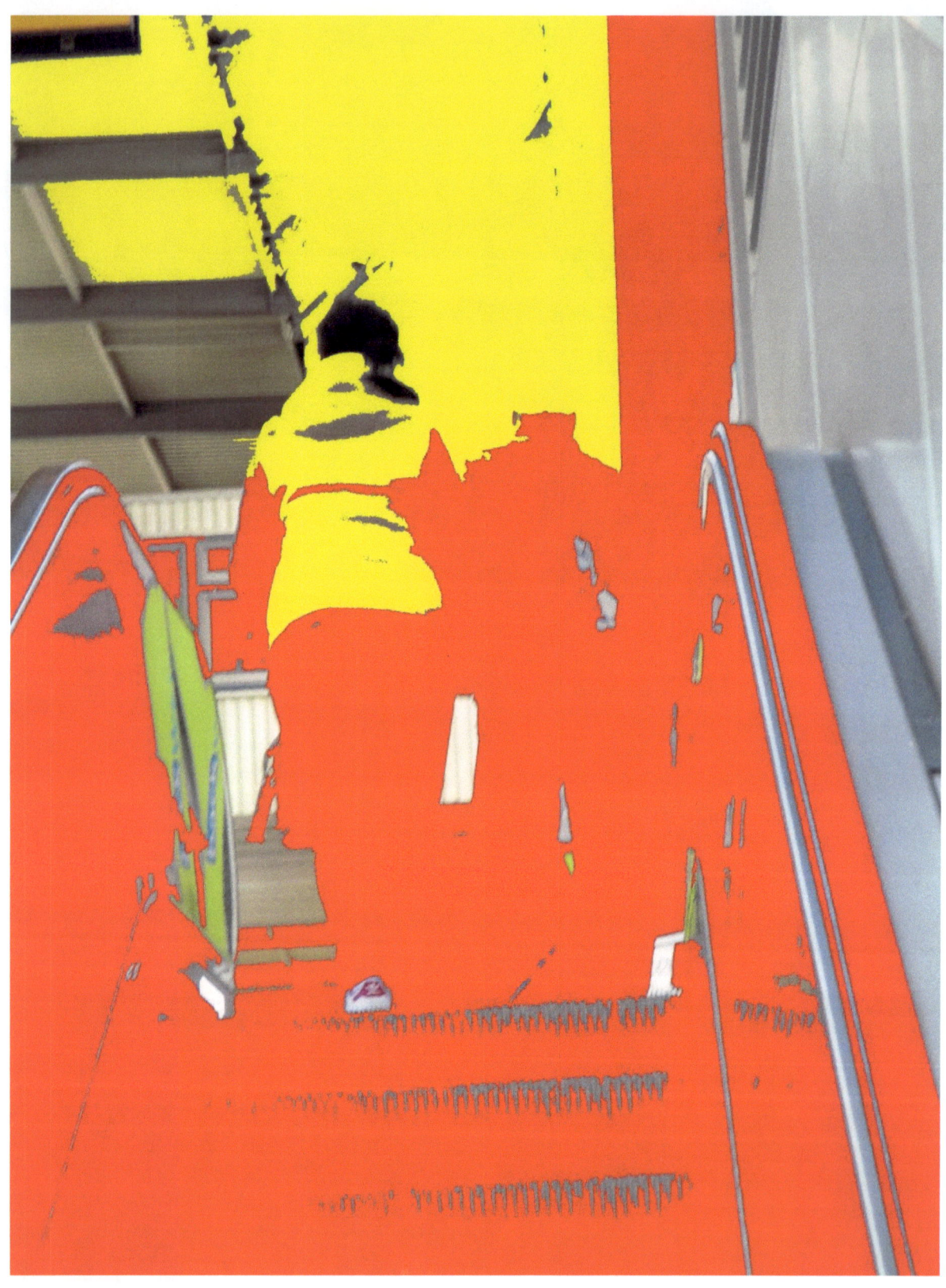

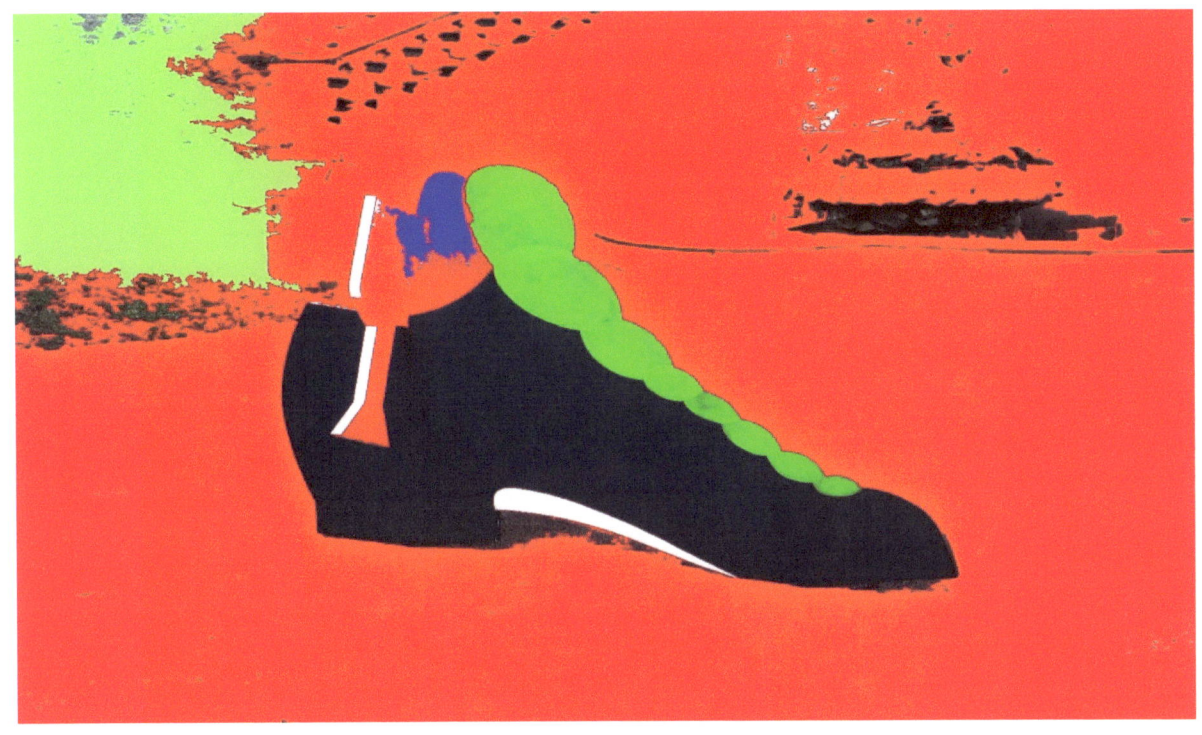
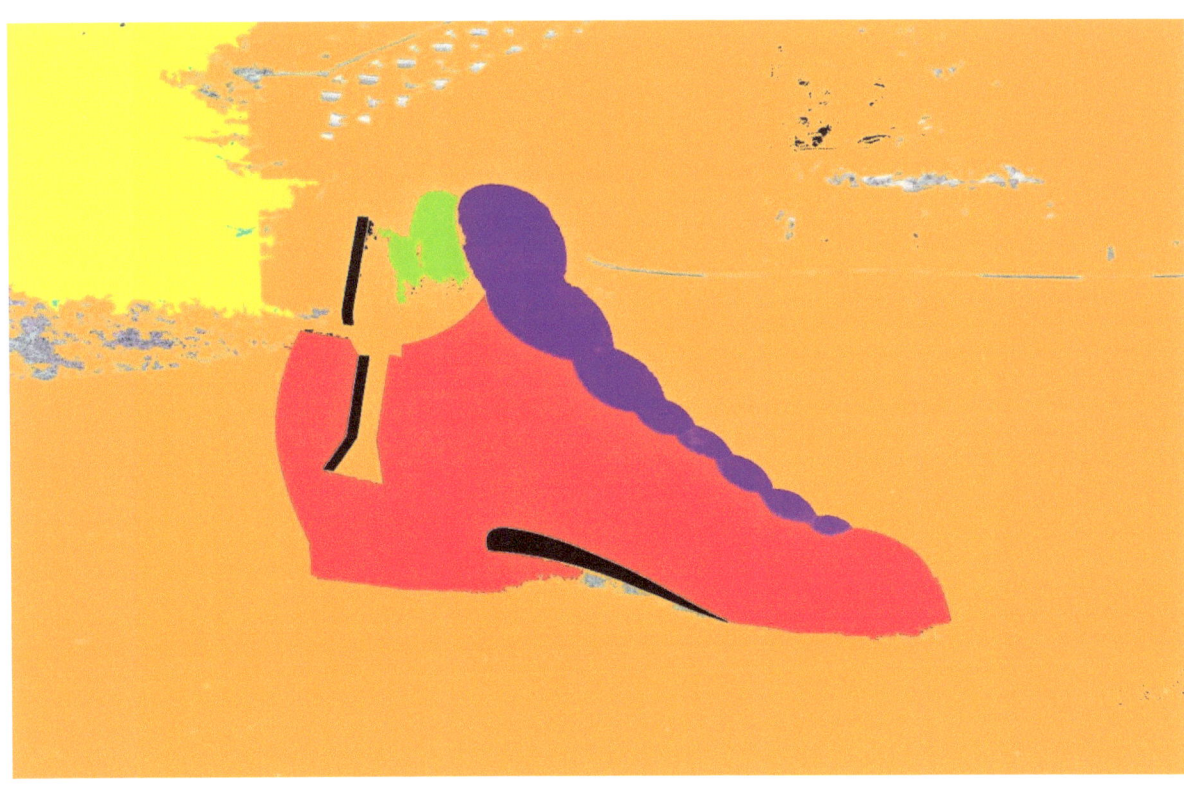

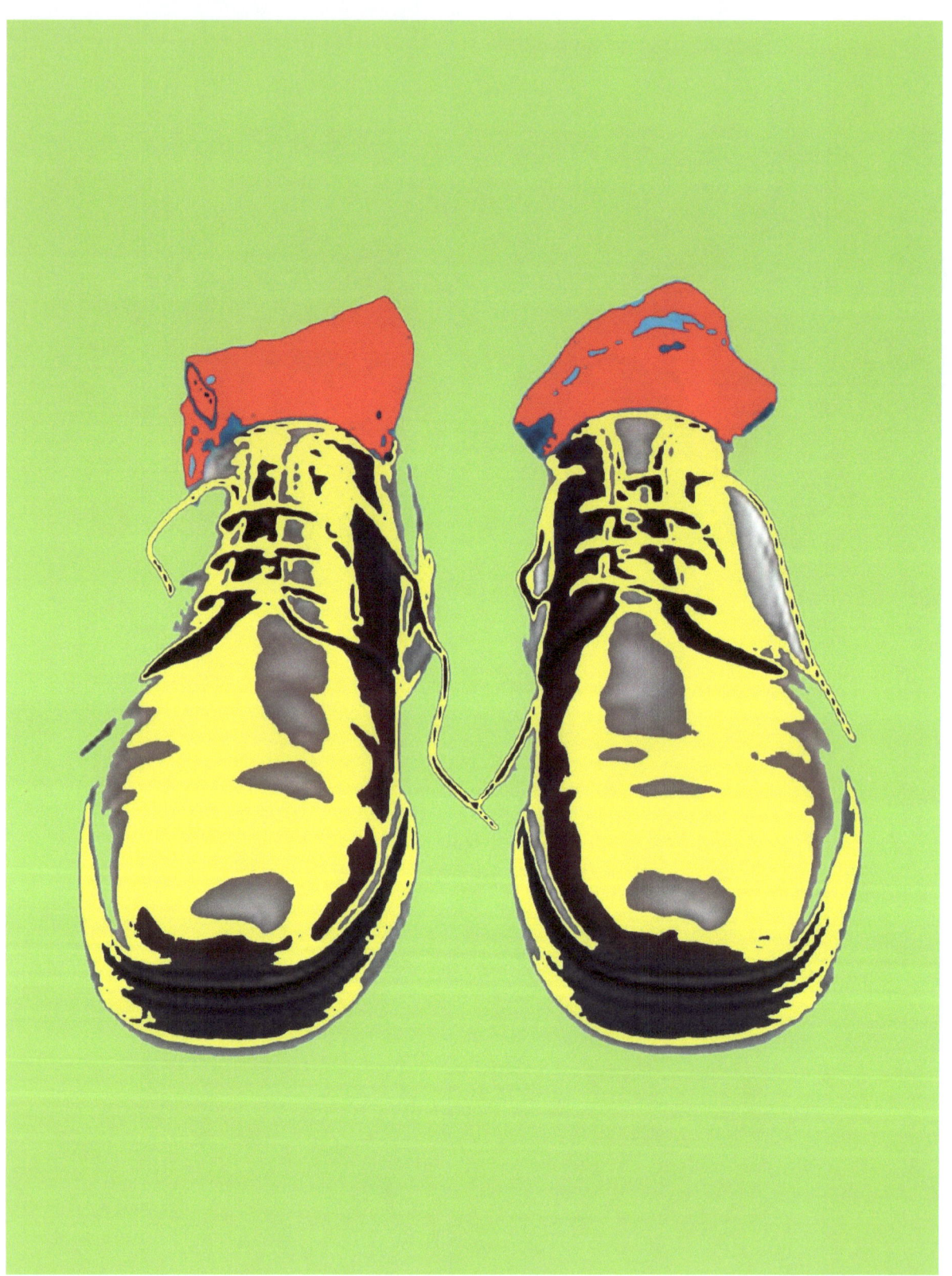

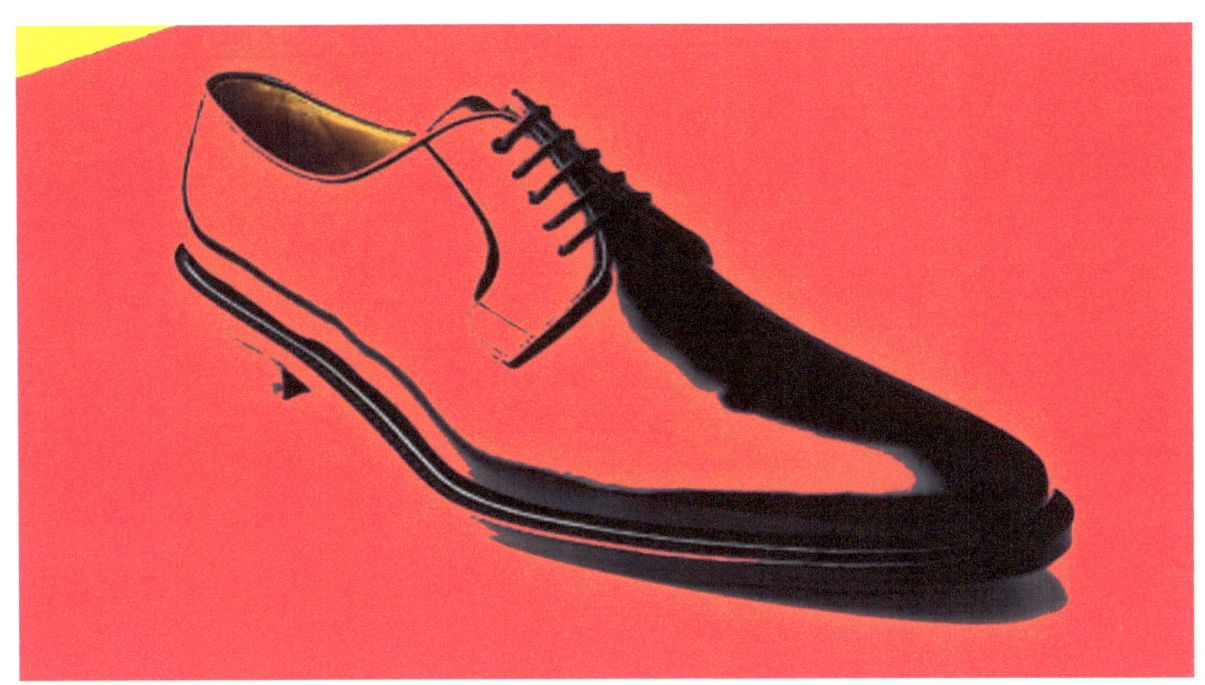

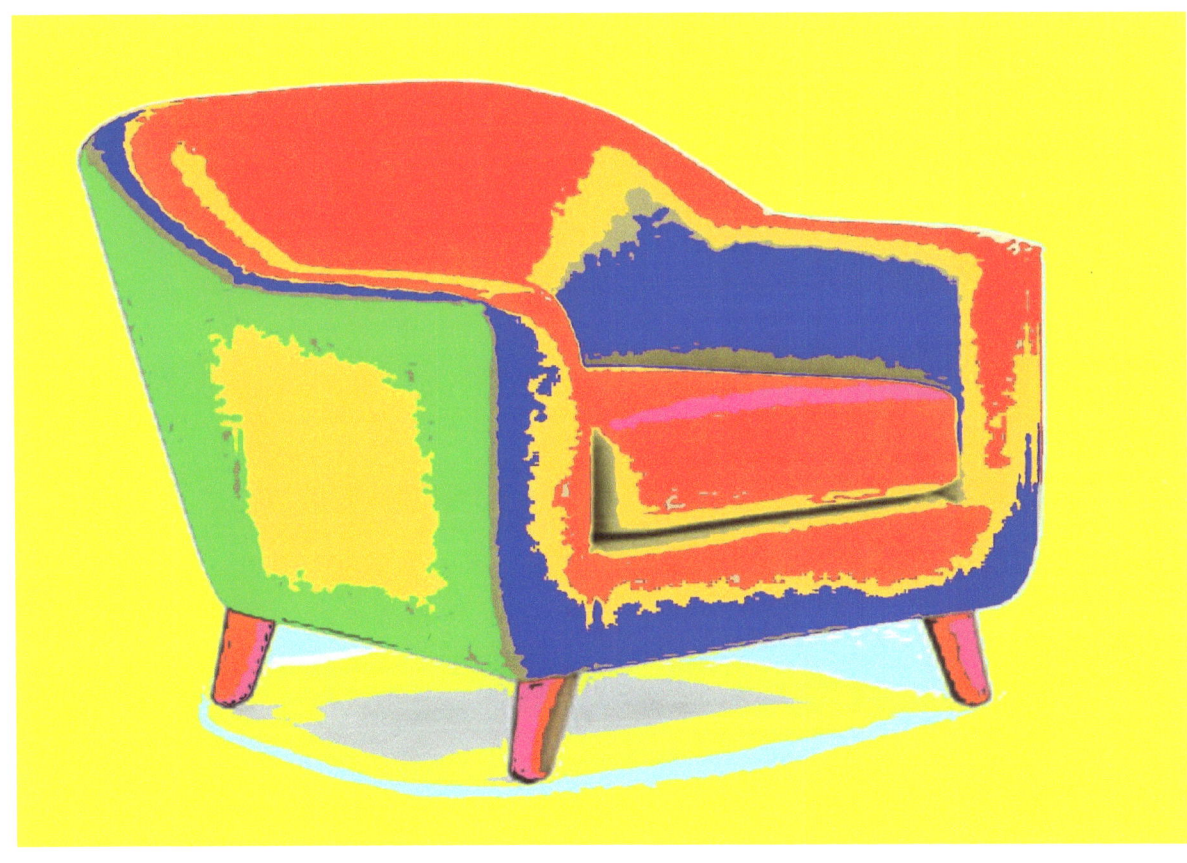

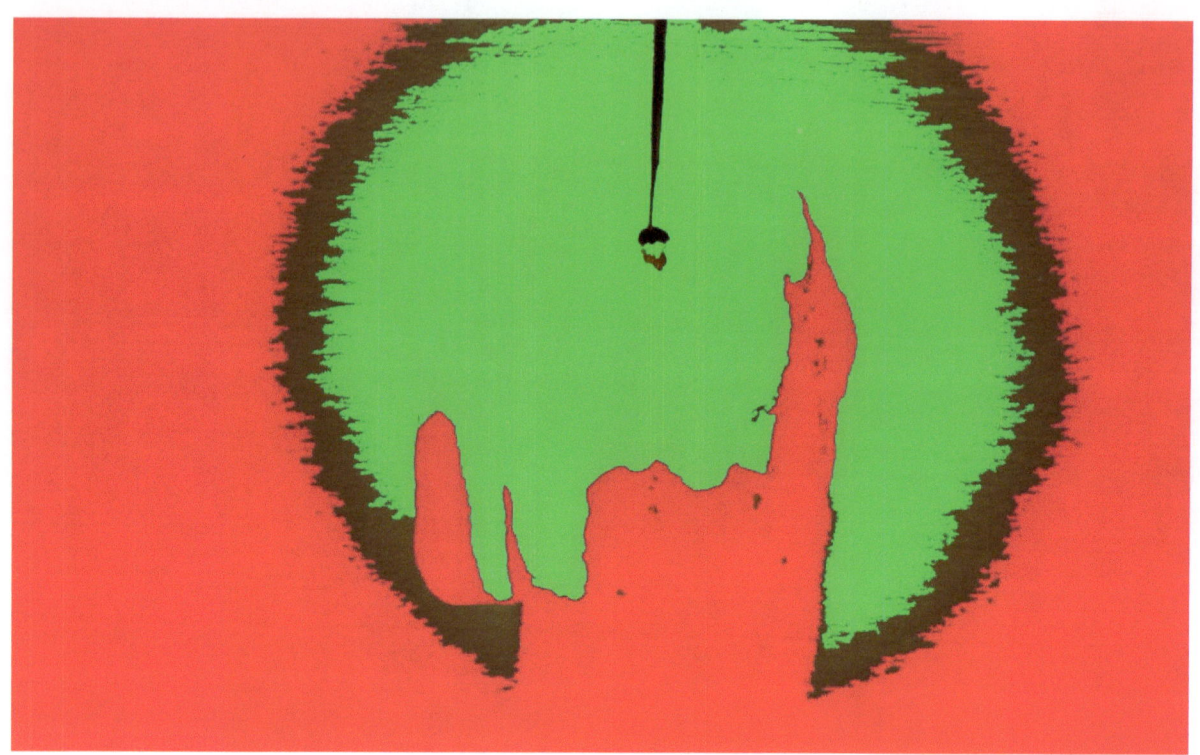
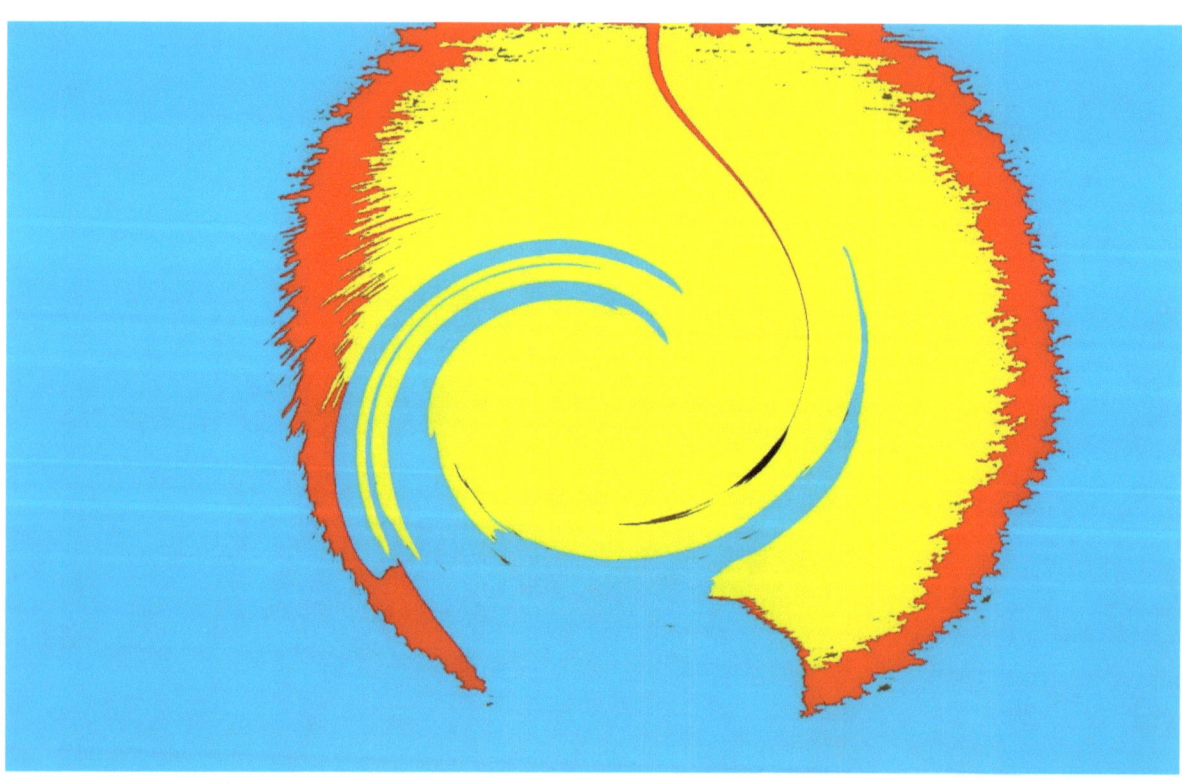

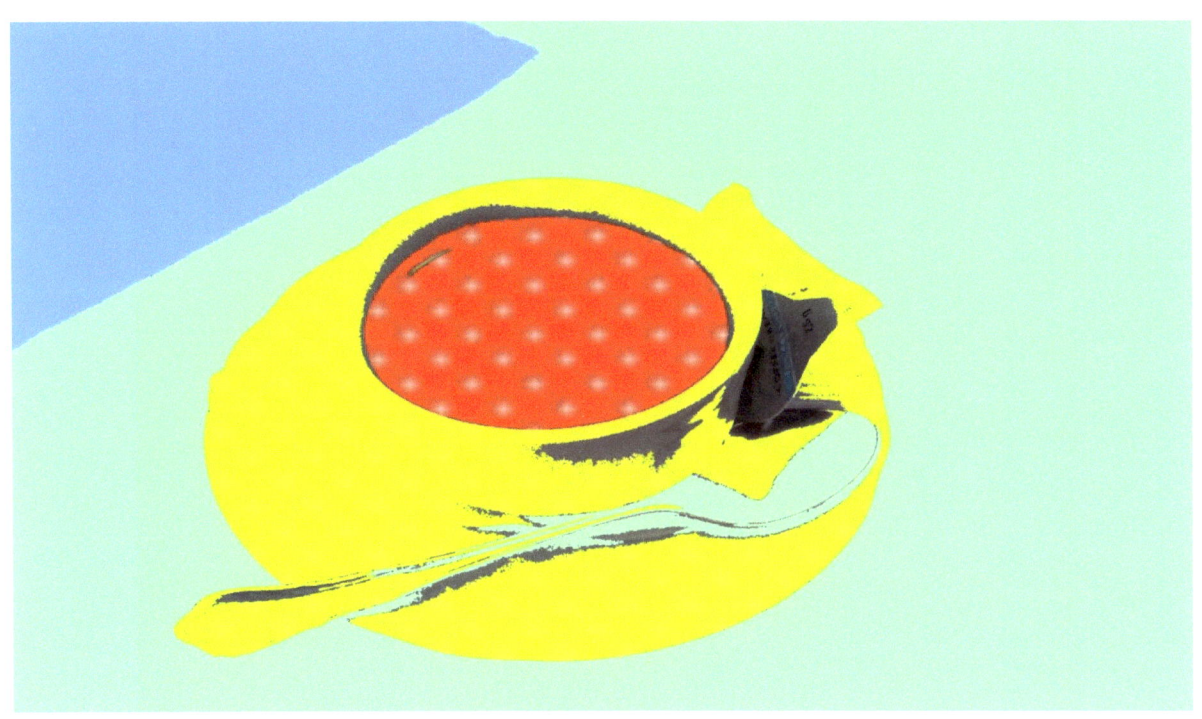
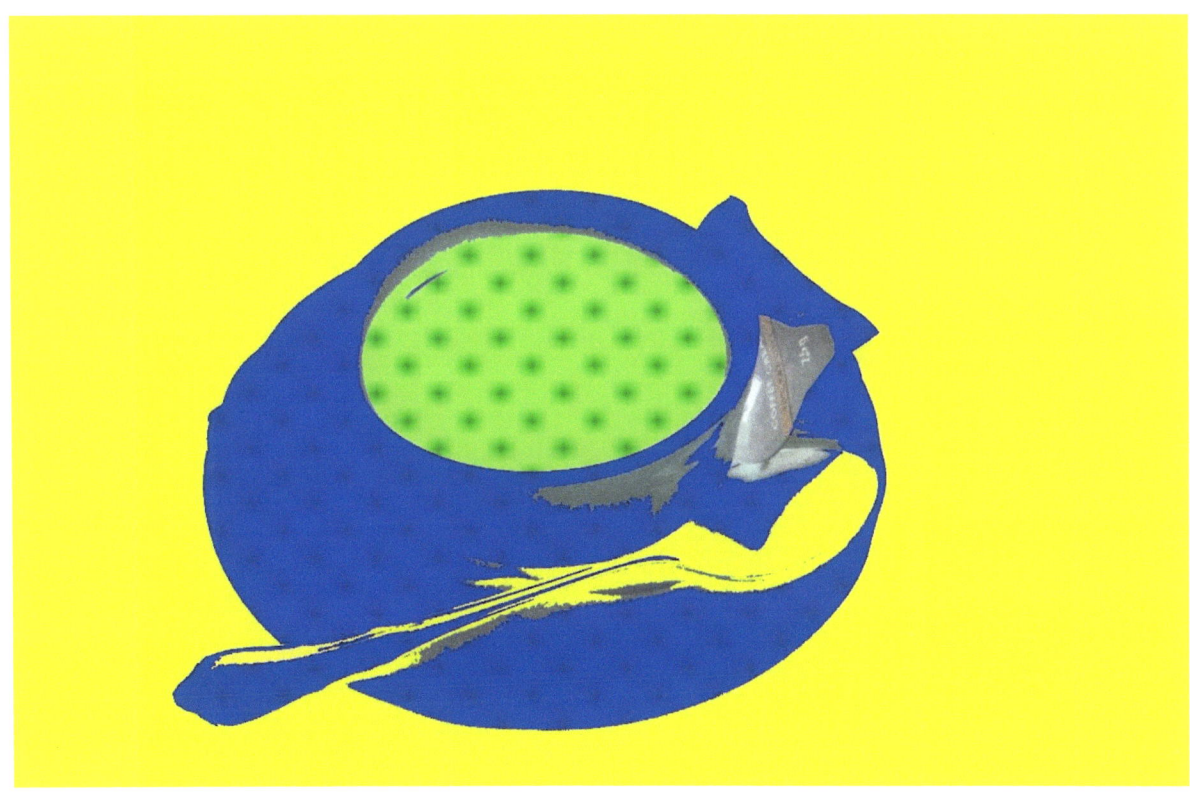

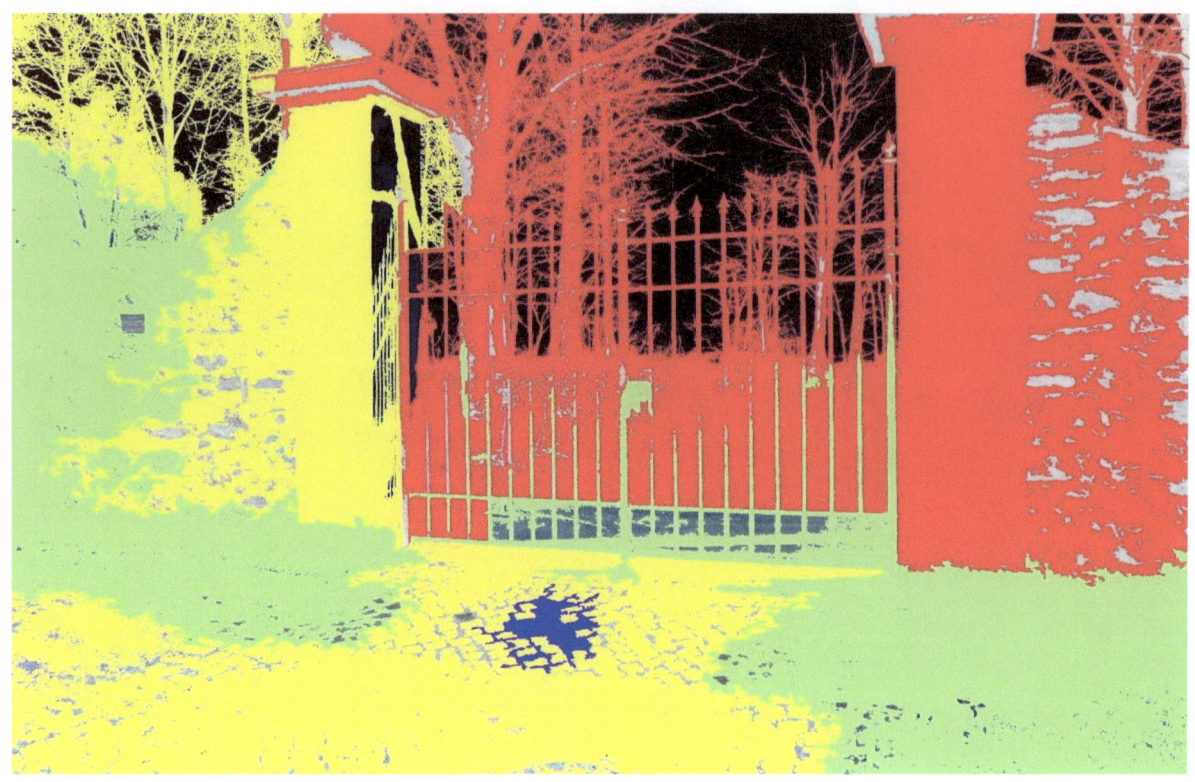
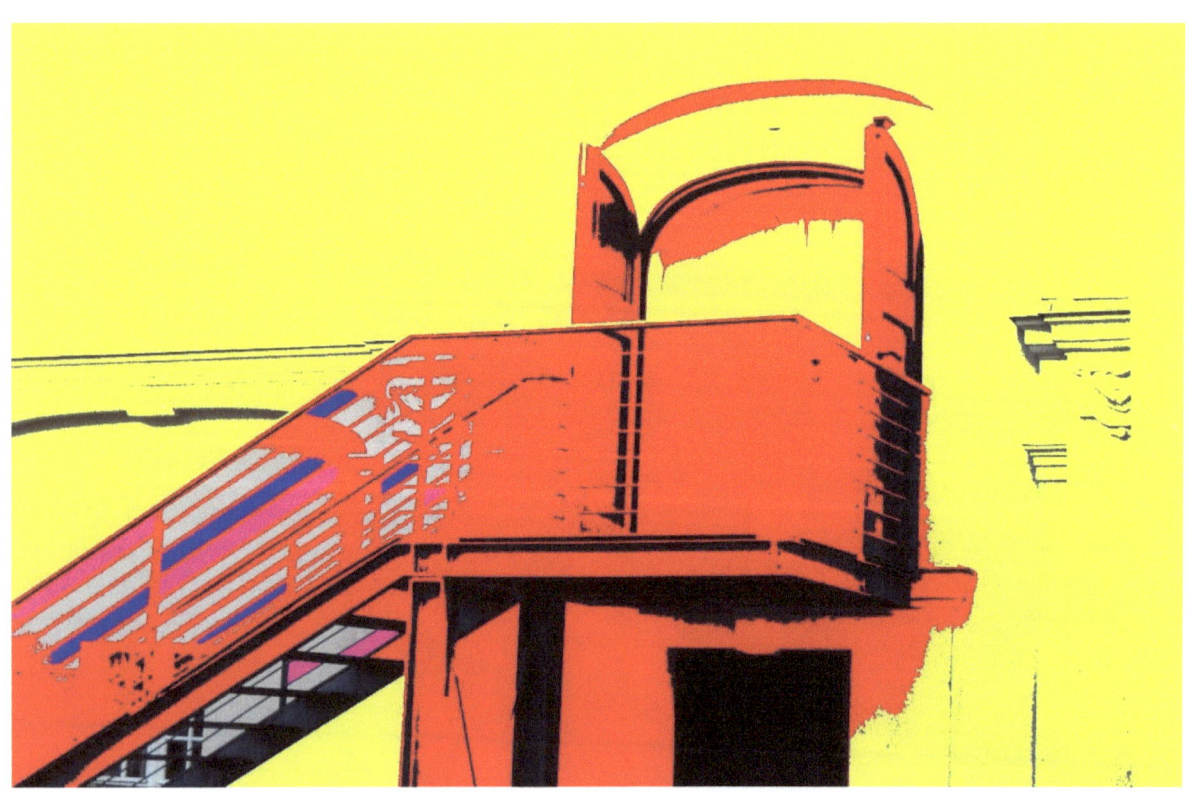

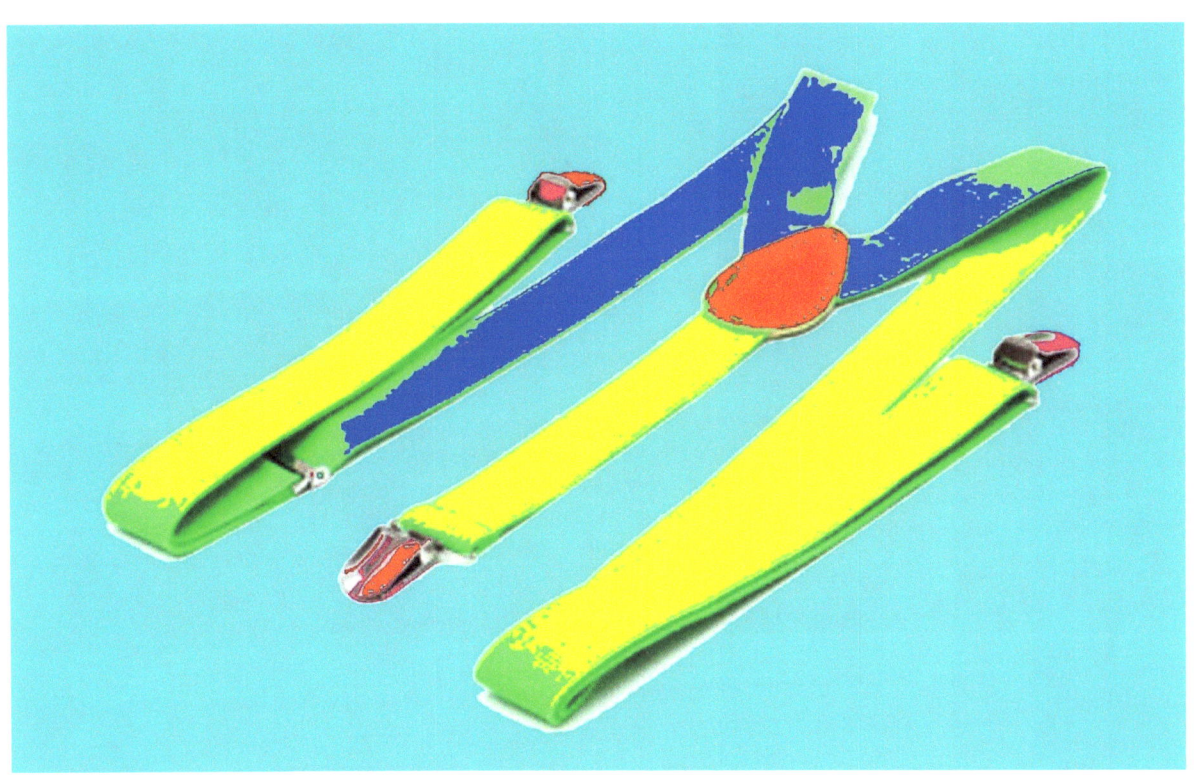
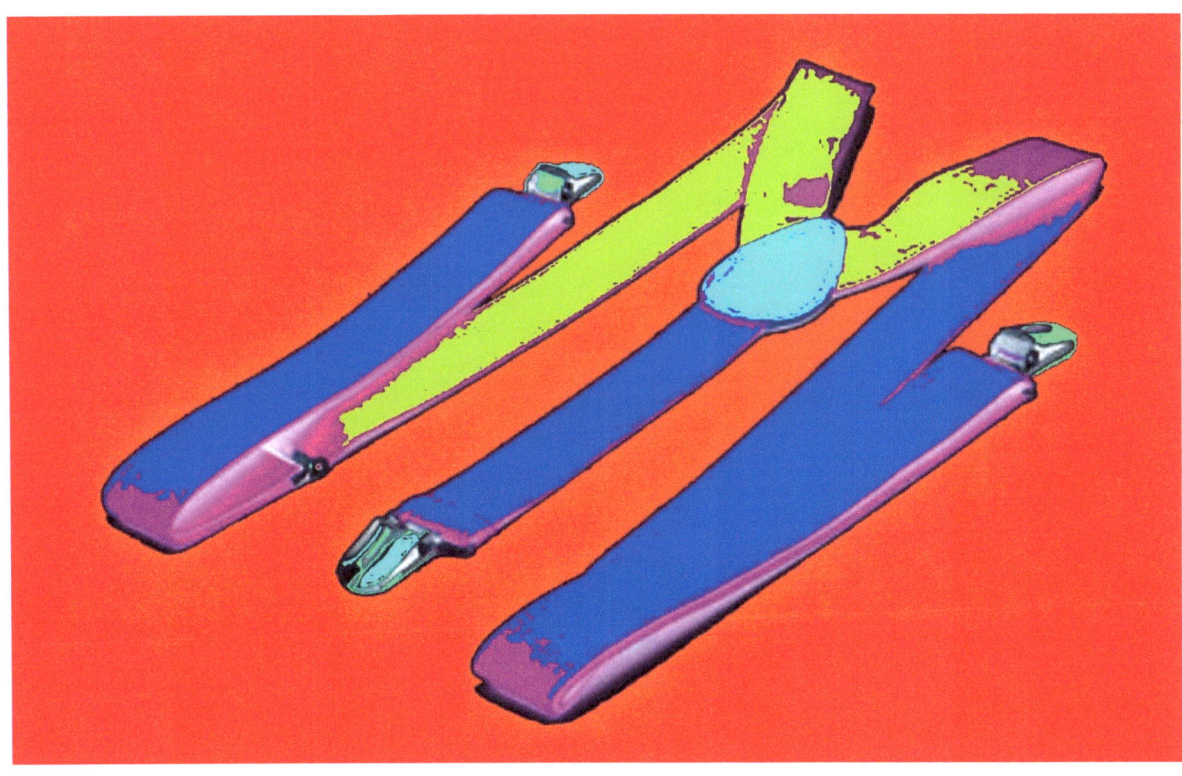

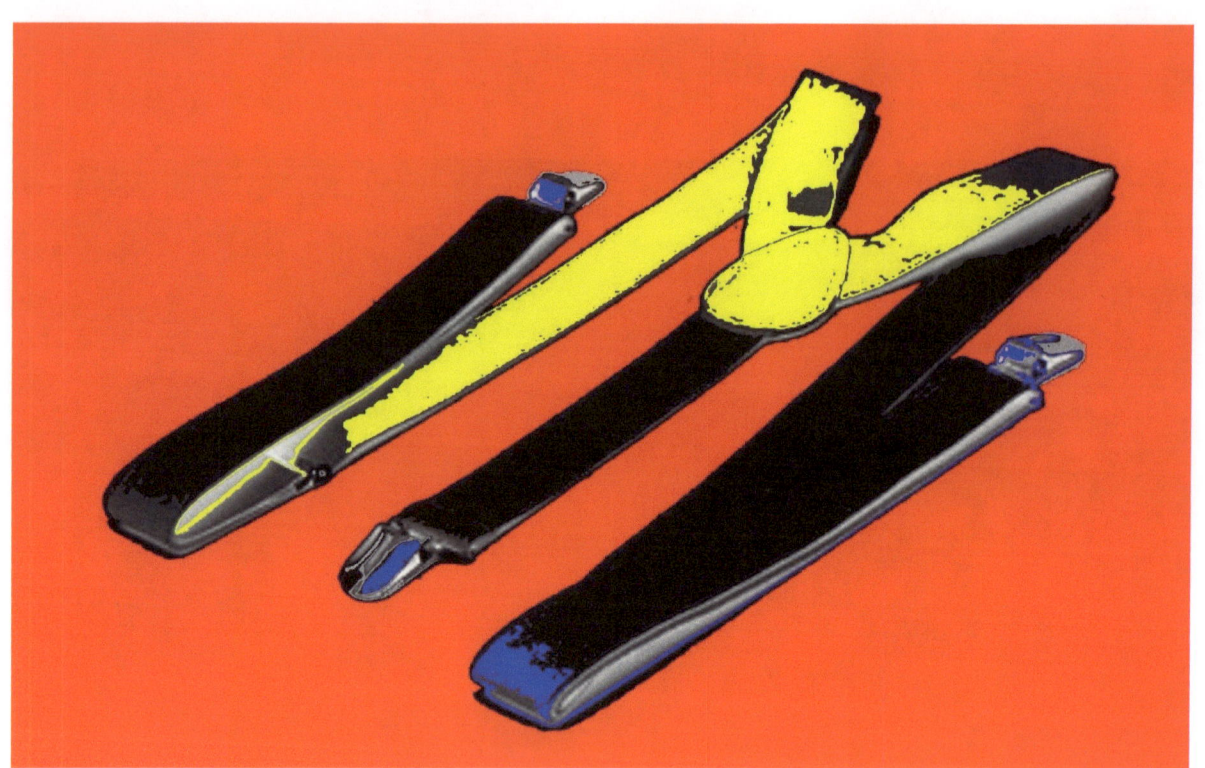
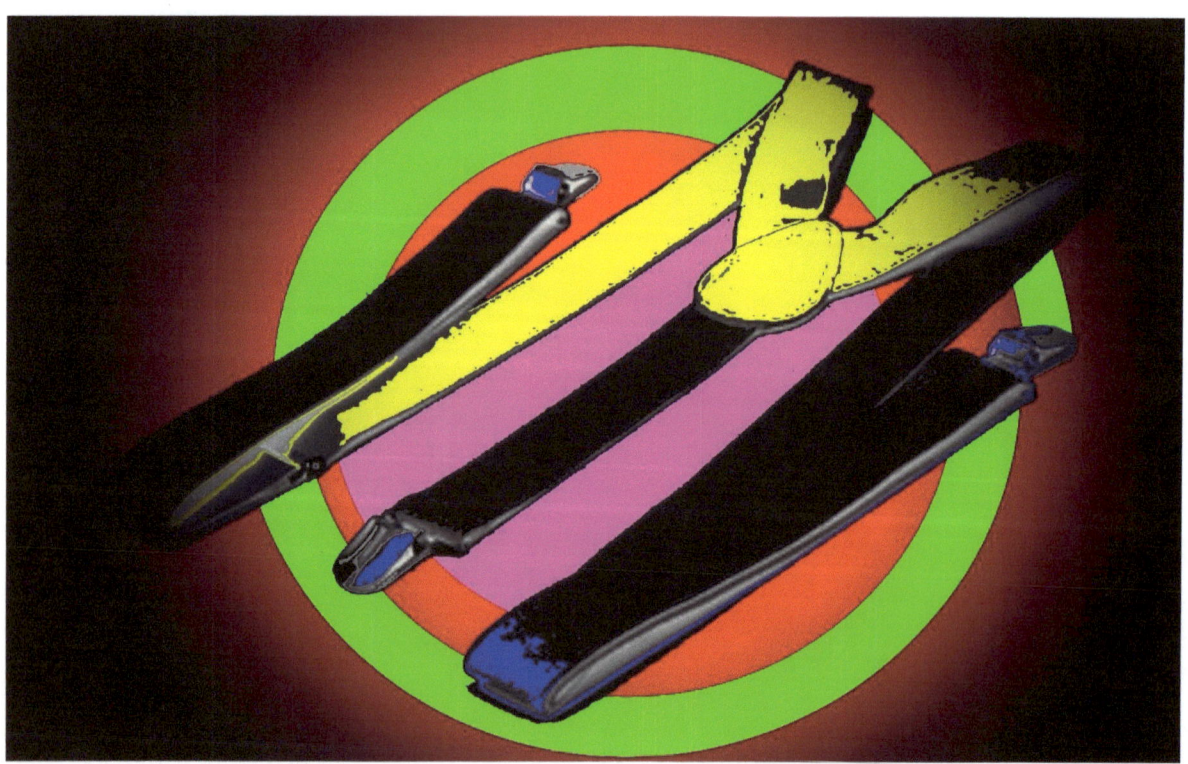

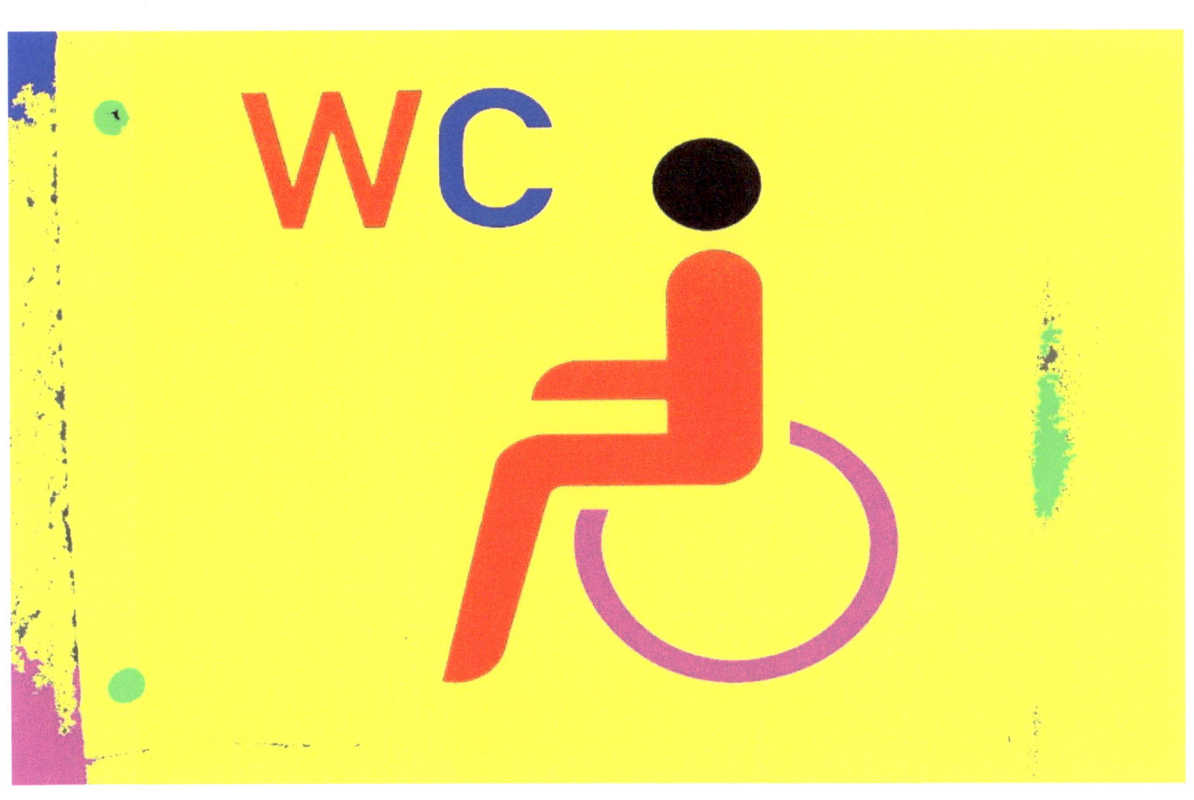

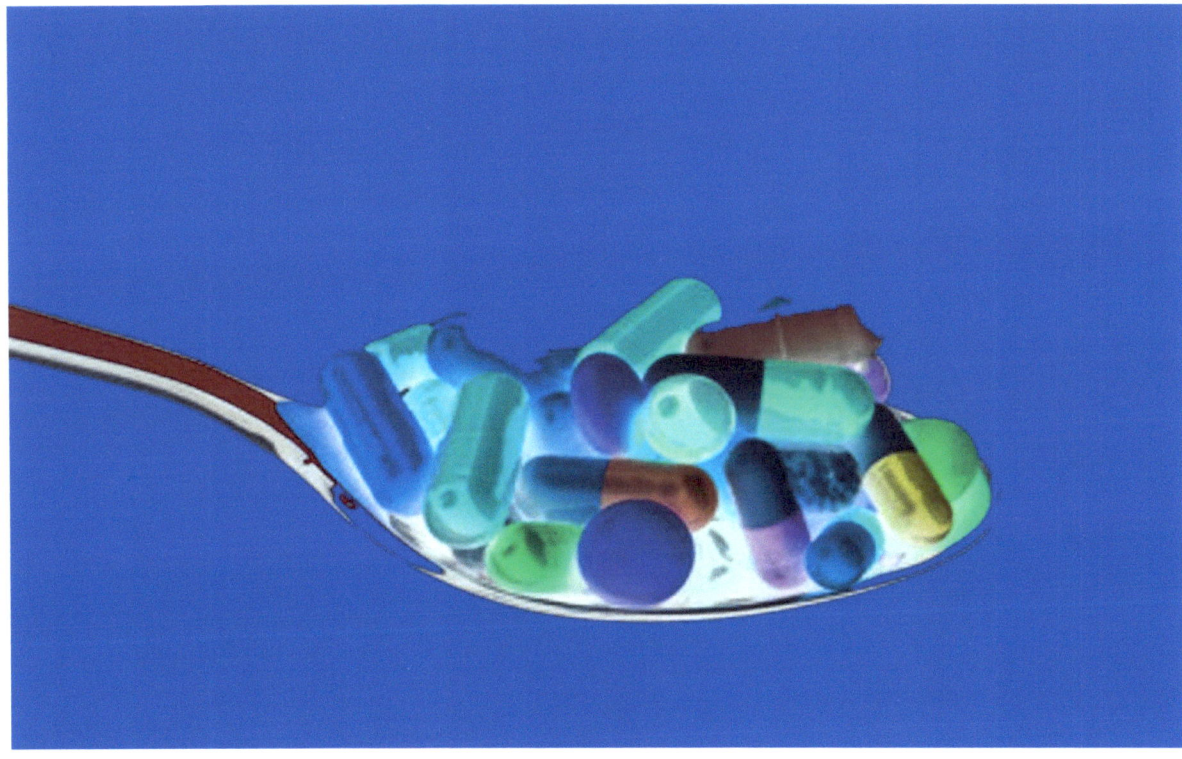

Anhang

Der Bildband POP ART NEW ist auch auf folgenden Verkaufskanälen als eBook erhältlich:

Amazon Kindle

Des Weiteren mit der ISBN:

978 – 3 – 9624 – 6403

Barnes & Noble

Casa del Libro

iBookstore

Kobo/Fnac

Weltbild, Hugendubel, Thalia, buch.de, buecher.de.

Donauland.at, Google Play Books, e-Sentral, Scribd

und einige mehr… .

www.ingramcontent.com/pod-product-compliance
Lightning Source LLC
Chambersburg PA
CBHW040453220526
45473CB00004B/1614